THE HUNTS

A history of the design, development and careers of the 86 destroyers of this class built for the Royal and Allied Navies during World War II

John English

To my wife Lynne without whose encouragement and support
this book would not have appeared

Published in 1987 by the World Ship Society, 28 Natland Road, Cumbria, England

ISBN 0 905617 44 4

Contents

Cover: GLAISDALE (R.N.N.) on completion at Liverpool 6.42
Frontispiece: HAYDON (10.42) This photograph is the original and must be compared with that on page 67,
which is the "doctored" view issued by the Ministry of Information   (N.M.M.)

ACKNOWLEDGEMENTS

Many thanks must be given to David Brown, Mike Mcaloon, Paul Melton and Arnold Hague of the Naval Historical Branch (NHB) for allowing me to consult their files. Further thanks must be given to David Lyons and Mr White of the Draft Room and Dennis Stonham and David Hodge of the photographic library of the National Maritime Museum (NMM). David Lyons must be further thanked for the use of a private article on the Hunt class. David Brown of the Royal Corps of Naval Constructors is thanked for the use of private papers on the development of the Hunt class, which he generously allowed me to use. Thanks also to Bill Bygraves for the use of his notes. Mr. Bill English is thanked for providing accommodation in London.

Moreover, I am greatly indebted to Ian Buxton, Richard Osborne and Michael Crowdy of the World Ship Society for their many suggestions for the improvement of the text. Thanks are also offered to my brother Peter and Huw Daniel for help with the photographs used in the book and to Jenny Thomas and Sylvia Black for typing and re-typing the manuscript. Ken Royall and Ian Buxton are thanked for the loan of photographs.

A NOTE ON SOURCES

The primary sources used in the production of the book were the records held at the NHB, the Ships Covers held in the Draft Room of the NMM that give the technical background of the class as well as some records held at the Public Records Office. Many secondary sources were also used, especially the *War at Sea* (Roskill), Rohwer's *Chronology of the War at Sea*, various editions of *Janes Fighting Ships* as well as specific books on the Arctic convoys and Malta convoys.

NOTE ON THE CATEGORIES OF RESERVE

On 15.1.44 the Reserve Fleet was re-instituted, under the Flag Office Commanding Reserve Fleet (FOCRF) who was responsible for arranging lay-up berths, for destoring and for the maintenance of ships in reserve. Originally three categories were defined:

(A) New Construction for which crews were not available.
(B) Ships, which would be required for further service.
(C) Ships unlikely to be commissioned for further service.

On 16.4.45 these three categories of Reserve were re-defined as follows:

(A) New construction for which crews are not at present available or which are not required for immediate service.
(B) Ships which will be required for further service. The notice at which they will be required for service to be decided by the Admiralty in each case.
(C) Ships unlikely to be commissioned for further service. Ships to be de-stored, de-equipped and the main and ancilliary machinery not to be preserved.

This system lasted for two years, until 16.5.47 when a revision was instituted:

A1 Operation Reserve 1: Ships to be fully maintained and at 14 days notice for full operational service.
A2 Operational Reserve 2: As above, but needing refit or docking to bring them up to 14 days notice for full operational service.
B1 Supplementary Reserve: Ships required in an emergency and maintained in a state fit for limited operational service on completion of a minor refit.
B2 Extended Reserve: Ships required in a future emergency to be preserved until required. Would require extensive refit before even entering limited service.
C   Disposal List: Ships not required for further service.

The Reserve Fleet nomenclature was again revised on 1.1.49 and was defined as follows:

Category A: Operational Reserve: Ships fit for full operational service within three months of mobilisation and if possible to be maintained at 30 days notice.
Category B: Supplementary Reserve: Ships required for operational service but will be required after Category A vessels.
Category C: Extended Reserve: Ships to be preserved for future employment. These vessels are not to be commissioned until after post-mobilisation expansion takes place.
Category Z: Disposal List: Ships no longer required for service.

This system was superceded on 7.11.52 by the following:

CLASS I: Ships free from important defects, stored and manned by a nucleus crew and at 14 days notice to proceed to work-up base.
CLASS II: As class I, but de-humified and at 30 days notice for readiness.
CLASS III: Ships at extended notice and requiring a refit before service.
CLASS IV: Ships no longer required for service.

The above scheme lasted until 1958, when the reserve categories were defined as:

OPERATIONAL RESERVE: Ships fully maintained and refitted. Two weeks notice.
SUPPLEMENTARY RESERVE: Required for specific purposes. Maintained in present state, normally stored but not normally refitted.
EXTENDED RESERVE: Ships which are destored, partially de-equipped and laid up without maintenance and ships approved for disposal.

The Reserve fleet concept was finally abandoned in the 1960's with the reduction in the size of the fleet and by the realisation that any future war would be of short duration.

GENESIS

In November 1918 the Royal Navy was in the happy position of having over 400 destroyers in service, with large numbers of the 'S', 'V/W' and Admiralty Leader classes still to complete, building or authorised. However many of these destroyers were cancelled at the end of the War and the remaining vessels of the three classes were completed in the years up to 1924. During the inter-war years all the wartime 'M' class, every 'R' except SKATE and many of the 'S' and 'V/W' classes were disposed of, so that by September 1938 only some 70 vessels of the 'R', 'S', 'V/W' and Admiralty leaders remained.

The development of fleet destroyers re-started in 1924 with the ordering of the prototypes AMAZON and AMBUSCADE. These vessels were a development of the Modified 'V/W' class and with successive minor improvements formed the basis for a series of over 70 vessels culminating in the commissioning of the 'I' class in 1937. The later classes — the Tribals, 'J', 'K', and the then projected 'L' classes — were responses to the large super destroyers being built for foreign navies. The Tribals, which were the largest destroyers yet to be built for the Royal Navy, carried eight 4.7″ guns but cost £700,000 each and clearly on grounds of cost could not be produced in large numbers. The subsequent 'J' and 'K' classes (completed in 1938/9) which were a smaller design mounting only six 4.7″ guns but with a large torpedo outfit were also expensive, costing £610,000 each. Furthermore they were not wholly suited to anti-submarine warfare and had been delayed because of problems with the delivery of their 4.7″ guns.

Thus in 1938, the Royal Navy had approximately 180 destroyers for fleet and escort duties built or building of which over 70 were over-age vessels. The disarmament policies that had been followed by governments of all persuasions, had resulted in these destroyer flotillas being acutely under strength.

In parallel with the development of Fleet destroyers, very limited funds had been made available to replace the World War I minesweeping and escort sloops of the Flower, Racehorse and Hunt classes. The Halycon class minesweepers had been built in small numbers during the late 1930's. Starting in 1929 with the Bridgewater class and developing through the succeeding Hastings, Shoreham, Falmouth, Grimsby and Fleetwood classes, the Royal Navy had arrived at a first rate convoy escort in the Egret/Black Swan classes then under construction. The Black Swans had the excellent anti-aircraft armament for 1938 of six 4″ high angle guns, with machine guns for close defence. However, their speed was limited to 19 knots, each vessel cost £470,000 to build and their fire control system was almost non-existent.

By 1938, it had become clear that war with Germany was inevitable and it was realised that the Royal Navy was facing an acute shortage of vessels suitable for both fleet and convoy duties. Ideally, the Royal Navy required a vessel with speed suitable for fleet duties combined with the armament of the Black Swans, and Mr A. P. Cole, Assistant Director of Naval Construction, in a memo to the Director of Naval Construction (DNC), Sir Stanley Goodall, outlined the current difficulties of building fleet destroyers, when large numbers of vessels were required for anti-submarine and anti-aircraft escort duties:

"The problem of the delivery of guns and mountings for Fleet Destroyers. The Dido and Fiji class cruisers of the 1936 and subsequent programmes had been delayed because of the inadequate gun-mounting production facilities available in Britain. It would take 39 months from the sketch design being approved to a Fleet destroyer being delivered, whilst delivery times for an escort vessel would be 30 months."

Thus, Cole demonstrated that a cheap, easily built, fast escort was a possible solution and the genesis of the Hunt class is to be seen in this memo.

Bottlenecks in the production of gun-mountings had become apparent by 1938. These meant that an off-the-shelf easily produced weapon had to be used for the escort vessels' main armament. The weapon selected was the Mark XVI 4″ HA/LA gun with Mark XIX twin mounting, which had been used successfully in the Egret class. For fleet operations, the proposed vessels would need a speed of at least 25 knots and this meant that they would require steam turbine machinery which, besides being expensive, called for still further use of the limited turbine-making facilities of the British marine engineering industry.

THE DESIGN OF TYPE 1 HUNTS

The considerations outlined above and the need to have the vessels in service quickly, meant that the six month design period of the ships was of necessity far shorter than normal.

Two preliminary sketch designs were drawn up for the DNC by two different constructors:

Constructor Hall produced:
'A' 810 tons (standard) 265' (waterline) × 27' × 17' depth (that is the distance between the keel and the main deck) with 4 × 4″ (2 × 2), 2MG (2 × 1), four torpedo tubes, 30 knots.

Whilst Constructor Bessant produced:
'B' 650 tons 240' (waterline) × 25' × 8'10″ (draught) 4 × 4″ (2 × 2), 2MG (2 × 1), four torpedo tubes, 25 knots.

Both designs made provision for depth charges.

Bessant aimed for a roll period of seven to eight seconds giving a GM of 2 ft at standard displacement. (GM is defined as the distance between the centre of gravity G, and the metacentre M, which can be regarded as an imaginary point of suspension. GM must be positive, but not so large as to give too short a roll period). The 30 knot design was estimated to cost £376,800 whilst the 25 knot design was estimated at £309,300. Both the designs were to be characterised by seaworthiness, the ability to carry up to 32 mines, mine sweeping gear and to have an endurance of 3,500 miles at 15 knots and 1,000 miles at 25 knots. However low cost was to be the primary objective.

On 28.9.38, these sketch designs were discussed by Admiral A. B. Cunningham (C in C Mediterranean), the Controller and Third Sea Lord, Admiral R. G. H. Henderson and the DNC (Goodall).

The following characteristics were agreed:

Speed to be 28/32 knots according to loading.

Armament to consist of six 4" HA/LA guns in three twin mountings.

Although there were to be no torpedo tubes or minesweeping equipment, the vessels were to be fitted with Asdic, depth charges and stabilisers.

The vessels were to be fitted with a bow form similar to the new 'J' class destroyers.

An alternative design mounting four 4" (2 × 2) and a triple set of torpedo tubes was to be considered and costed.

This was nearer to the design developed by Hall; however Goodall decided that as Bessant was more experienced, he should develop the design.

Subsequently, the design was amended to take into account suggestions made on 14.10.38., that the proposed ships be lengthened by 20 ft to accommodate the larger crew which it was now estimated would be required to man these vessels. The DNC agreed to lengthen the vessels but by only 7 ft to improve habitability, trim and to provide a margin for contingencies. As a result the Hunts were to become notorious for being overcrowded and weight critical and it seems clear that they could have been better vessels if the extra 13 ft had been retained.

Bessant then went through the component weights of the design and the calculation of the height of the vessel's centre of gravity (KG), that had originally been estimated by Hall, and Bessant's estimate showed no significant difference from Hall's quick estimate.

Goodall then reviewed the whole calculations and in his diary of 17.10.38. records:

"Went through escort design. Ship too big. Hall is inexperienced".

The next day he re-considered his views and recorded:

"Altered yesterday's decisions on escorts and put in 7 ft (on the length) to give margins".

It would seem that the DNC had forgotten that Bessant was working to 272' rather than the 265' discussed at the Controller's meeting. Goodall was approving a fait accompli. At the same time Goodall asked his staff to investigate the effect on ship sizes of three variations to the basic design. The anticipated results were as follows:

Variation	Effect on Size	Effect on Cost	Effect on Complement
1 Reduce speed from 29/32 knots to 27/30 knots	Reduction of 25 tons in displacement	Saving of £16,000	Nil
2 Reduce the armament from six to four 4"	Reduction of 90 tons in displacement	Saving of £40,000	Complement reduced by 25
3 Increase endurance from 3,000 to 4,000 miles (would require 75 tons of oil)	Increase in displacement of 125 tons Deep displacement 200 tons Increase in SHP by 3,000	Increase of £50,000	Nil

This shows that a better vessel could have been constructed with longer endurance but at greater cost. The raison d'etre of the class was that these vessels would be constructed quickly and cheaply. By this time, the proposed armament had been increased by providing 30 depth charges and a Type 128 Asdic was to be installed with a housing dome. Power had been increased to maintain 29 knots in the deep condition ($33\frac{1}{2}$ knots in standard condition) with endurance of 2,500 miles at 20 knots. The complement was now six officers and 137 ratings.

On 22.10.38, the First Sea Lord Sir Roger Backhouse approved more of the characteristics of the vessels:
Endurance was to be 2,500 miles at 20 knots.

The officers' quarters were to be forward. The Hunts were the first destroyer type vessels to have accommodation so arranged and this arrangement was to become a standard feature on all future destroyer construction, as it provided easy access to the bridge.

No 1 gun was to be situated on a platform raised 18″ above the forecastle to give the position extra protection from the sea.

No bullet proof plating was to be fitted, nor was elaborate wireless telegraphy to be provided.

In November, the GM was calculated as 2.42 ft at standard displacement and 2.55 ft when deep loaded. This compared well with the GM of interwar destroyers. However, at this time there occurred an indicator of the weight problems that were to arise later. The constructors estimated the weight of the hull at 457 tons, whereas a team of draughtsmen carrying out a detailed weight calculation from structural drawings worked out the volume of steel at each frame giving an estimated hull weight of 495 tons. This calculation was not accepted as it was believed that the team of calculators had allowed for heavier scantlings than required.

On 29.11.38 the following Legend of Particulars was presented to the Admiralty Board for the new "Fast Escort Vessels" of the 1939 programme:

(At this time, the Hunts were referred to as Fast Escort Vessels to overcome Treasury reluctance to build an extra 20 destroyers).

Dimensions:	Length: 278 ft (overall), 272 ft (waterline), 264 ft (between perpendiculars)
	Breadth: 28 ft 3 in
	Draught 7 ft 11 in (light)
Displacement:	890 tons (standard) 1,185 tons (deep load).
Armament:	6 × 4″ (3 × 2) Mk XVI, two machine guns, two depth charge throwers
Complement:	Between 142-144 officers and men
Endurance:	2,500 miles at 15 knots

The estimated weights at this time were:

General Equipment	58 tons
Machinery	270 tons
Armament and Ammunition	87 tons
Hull	450 tons
Stabiliser	25 tons
Standard Displacement	890 tons
Oil Fuel and Reserve Feed Water	295 tons
Deep Displacement	1,185 tons

Two days later the sketch design and the Legend of Particulars were given Board approval and it was now estimated that each vessel would cost £400,000.

Subsequently, on 13.12.38, a Board Minute gave the order of priority of the ships to receive the 4″ Mk XIX gun mounting:

Priority 1	Five 'V/W' conversions
Priority 2	20 1939 Programme Fast Escort Vessels
Priority 3	36 'V/W' conversions

On 30.12.38 Rear-Admiral Burroughs, the Assistant Chief of the Naval Staff (ACNS) noted that approval had been given to order ten vessels of the class. However, orders for the second ten vessels were to be delayed pending the evaluation of the alternative design with two twin 4″ and one triple/quadruple torpedo tube mounting.

This design variant was shown to have the following effects: increase displacement by seven tons, complement by one man and cost by £18,000 whilst the speed would be reduced by 0.1 knot, endurance by 20 miles and GM by 0.04 feet.

It is interesting to note that the staff requirement for the 1939 Fast Escort Vessel (ADM 1/9440) drawn up at this time was written around the original 'Hunt' class design and detailed the following roles for the vessels:

To supplement existing escort vessels on A/S and A/A escort duties.

To provide greater numbers of vessels for A/S and A/A escorts for fast transports and detached units of the Fleet.

For use at home and abroad.

Although primarily designed for wartime requirements, they could be used for training in peacetime.

They were to be capable of operating in any weather, with an endurance of 3,500 miles at 15 knots and 2,500 miles at 20 knots. Maximum speed was to be 29 knots in deep condition. Armament was to be 6 × 4″ (HA/LA), one quadruple two pounder and torpedo tubes (excepting the first ten). The vessels were to carry two depth charge throwers and 30 depth charges.

INITIAL BUILDING PROGRAMME

On 20.12.38 tenders for the construction of the first ten Fast Escort Vessels were invited, and these were to be received by 20.1.39 (a bit quicker than today!)

In an article on the design of Hunt class destroyers, D. K. Brown (chronicler of RCNC history) wrote: "On 8.2.39 the building drawings were sent for Board Approval and simultaneously to the builders. All the firms said that the Engineer-in-Chief's estimate of 270 tons for machinery was 30 tons too low. It was agreed to use 285 tons. The legend weight of the hull was 450 tons (despite the detailed calculation of 495 tons). The ship-builders suggested 475 tons and a figure of 460 was agreed with a margin of 10 tons. However as steel mills were required to roll all plates to the specified thickness or less, while the detailed calculation used the specified thickness throughout, there was real justification for using a figure lower than that of the detailed calculation."

At a meeting with the builders on 31.1.39, the builders stated that to build the vessels in mild steel and omitting galvanising would only save £3,000. The builders agreed to use 'D' quality steel and to galvanise without extra cost. This resulted in a saving of 13 tons in hull weight leaving the design 22 tons overweight compared with the revised hull weight of 460 tons.

Detailed calculations of the centre of gravity and weight was, by departmental instruction, always carried out by two calculators working separately. Only on completion of their work were the two answers compared. In the case of the Hunts, there was unusually close agreement. It would seem that these figures were accepted by the head of section even though the centre of gravity of the hull was now calculated as 0.8 ft lower than Bessant had estimated.

Goodall inspected the calculations on 9.2.39 and noted in his diary: "Looked at escort stability with new hull weights, not good enough. No margin, but must accept it".

However, he thought again and after a call from Yarrow's confirmed that the stability of the escorts was not good enough, Goodall decided to increase the beam.

The effect of a 6" increase in beam was reported to DNC on 13.2.39 and he asked for a further 3". On the 14th a decision was made to increase the beam from 28'3" to 29'. The shipyard overseers were informed by letter on 15.2.39. Both constructors and Goodall agreed to the change.

The extra beam increased the hull weight by five tons and the fuel load by 7 tons — the tanks got bigger. The speed was reduced by 0.1 knots due to the increased beam.

The DNC was not to be concerned in any further overall assessment of weight or stability until February 1940 following ATHERSTONE's inclining experiment.

On 14.3.39 the First Sea Lord directed that in order to speed production, the second batch of ten vessels were to be repeats of the first ten. A week later the first ten were ordered, to be followed quickly by the ordering of the second batch of ten some three weeks later on 11.4.39.

The cost of the vessels at this time (excluding armament, ammunition and dockyard materials which were supplied by the Admiralty), was quoted by the successful tenderers:

Builder	Vessel 1	Vessel 2
Cammell-Laird	£287,060	£286,750
John Brown	£285,630	£285,630
Swan Hunter & Wigham Richardson	£284,960	£283,960
Parsons Marine Steam Turbine/ Vickers Armstrongs (Tyne) (Hull)	£284,630	£284,380
Yarrows	£284,410	£284,100

The cost of machinery averaged £140,000 per unit or nearly 50% of the total cost of each vessel.

The first units of the class were laid down on 8.6.39 which was the earliest date that vessels of this type could be laid down, without breaking Treaty obligations. Progress was rapid with 18 of the first 20 vessels being laid down before the declaration of war and ATHERSTONE, HAMBLEDON and EGLINTON being launched before 1939 had closed.

ATHERSTONE'S STABILITY PROBLEMS

ATHERSTONE, the first of the class, was nearing completion and an inclining experiment was planned as usual to check the weight and centre of gravity of the completed ship. It would seem that when the detailed calculation had been repeated a serious error had been discovered in the previously calculated figures. Both the head of section and two constructors were at Cammell-Laird's for the experiment. Goodall noted in his diary on 7.2.40: "Cole came in with ATHERSTONE's inclining results. GM 1 ft less than calculated, bad error in calculation, shall have to do something drastic. S and B* to return at once to decide what is to be done... Calculations to be made leaving out gun and ballasting, also giving more beam."

Authors Note: the two constructors.

Bessant noted the reasons in his work book, the same day:

1. "An original error in preliminary calculations for the KG of the hull structure and fittings" (It seems that a slip was made in calculating the height of the centre of gravity (the upperdeck was taken at 7 feet above the keel instead of 17 feet) and this was not noticed because the ship was much smaller than previous destroyers). This was responsible for the two-thirds loss in stability.
2. Vessels turned out to be 60-70 tons heavier than estimated. They were 22 tons heavier than the final calculation and showed about 3" less GM than the final calculation. This was responsible for the other one-third loss of stability."

ATHERSTONE in 8.43, whilst serving with the Mediterranean Fleet. She is armed with four 4" guns, but originally she was to have shipped six 4" guns, but stability problems meant that a twin mounting was suppressed
(Brownell Collection)

It was calculated that 1,200 tons/ft would have to be recovered in order to restore stability. It was suggested that the first 20 vessels be altered in the following ways to reduce the centre of gravity:
(1) Land No 2 4" twin mount.
(2) Cut down after superstructure and other top weight including funnel and bridge.
(3) Fit 52 tons of permanent ballast.

The Group 1 vessels were thus armed on commissioning with 4 × 4", two machine guns plus two depth charge throwers.

In fact 23 vessels had to be altered this way, as three vessels of the second group BLENCATHRA, BROCKLESBY and LIDDESDALE were already too far advanced to be widened and so received modifications similar to those of the first group.

Group 2 vessels had their beam increased by 2'6" to 31'6" and recovered their stability in this way. It is believed that some units were 'kippered' on the slip to incorporate the required beam, which was achieved by widening shell strakes.

It would seem that the stability problems that arose in ATHERSTONE were a result of the pressure being placed on the naval constructors during 1938 and 1939. Supervision was inadequate and the head of section must be to blame for not checking the design of the new class against that of the BLACK SWAN's which were being designed in the same room and were also armed with three twin 4" mounts but on a beam of 37 ft. It is surprising that the head of section did not probe into the difference in the beams of the two designs. Secondly, there were inadequate checks on the weight of the individual parts to be used in the design and it is likely that this was due to the pressure of work on the constructors. Sometimes preliminary estimates scaled from existing designs could be more accurate than detailed estimates synthesised from the sum of calculated weights of components. Errors are always likely to occur when design is carried out in a hurry as happened with the Hunts.

THE TYPE 2 VESSELS

These 36 vessels were ordered under the 1939 War Emergency Programme. The first batch of 20 was ordered on 4.9.39 and 5.9.39 and was followed on 20.12.39 by the other 16. To speed production they were ordered as repeats of the original group. However, this group, except the three vessels mentioned earlier, incorporated the following alterations to the original design to improve stability:-

1. The beam was increased to 31 ft 6 in
2. The bridge was lowered and set further aft
3. The funnel was lowered. Deflectors, with restriction plates in the funnel, were fitted in order to reduce the amount of exhaust gases being swept over the bridge, as this had been a problem with the Type I vessels.

The result of these modifications was that the stability of vessels was significantly improved and no permanent ballast was shipped.

By early 1941, when the first of the Type 2's were being completed, the deficiencies of the anti-aircraft provision in all types of warships had been realised and resulted in their being fitted with quadruple two pounder (pompom) and two single 20 mm. Oerlikon guns in single mountings, when the latter weapons became available.

The resulting specification of the Type 2's was as follows:

Length: 280' (overall) 264' (pp)
Beam: 31'6"
Draught (standard): forward 9', aft 13' (over propellers)
Displacement: 1,050 tons (standard) 1,430 tons (deep)
Power on two shafts: 19,000 SHP
Max speed (deep load): 25 knots
Endurance: 2,560 miles at 20 knots. (In service this figure dropped to 1,550 miles)
Complement: Nine officers, 155 ratings (war)

The revised group weights of the Type 2's were as follows:

Hull	595 tons
Machinery	295 tons
Armament	136 tons
Equipment	111 tons
Oil Fuel	277 tons
RFW	16 tons
Deep Displacement	1,430 tons

The armament of the vessels was:

6 — 4" HA/LA in twin mounts.
1 — 2 pdr pompom (quadruple)
2 — 20 mm (2 × 1) Oerlikon
50 depth charges with one rail and two throwers.

THE TYPE 3 VESSELS

By the time discussions took place between the Naval Staff and the DNC in the spring of 1940 concerning the vessels to constitute the 1940 War Emergency Programme, it had become clear that the Hunts would be undertaking duties that had formerly belonged to fleet destroyers. Another design change was therefore initiated to ship a torpedo armament aboard the proposed vessels, albeit at the expense of a reduced gun armament. This proposal was in effect a revival of the idea to arm the second batch of ten vessels of the 1939 Programme with torpedoes.

At a meeting on 26.3.40 to discuss the proposed Type 3 design the following parameters were accepted:

1. The ships were to have a beam of $31\frac{1}{2}$ ft and a speed of 27 knots in deep loaded condition (which was greater than that of the Type 2's).
2. The quarterdeck 4" mounting was to be suppressed.
3. The vessels were to carry three depth charge chutes and four depth charge throwers with 100 depth charges, but it was accepted that two throwers only might have to be provided. (Generally two depth charge chutes, four throwers and 70 depth charges were carried).
4. Protection for the depth charge personnel was to be provided abaft the after superstructure.
5. Bullet proof protection was to be provided to the bridge and wheelhouse. To compensate for this, the bandstand under the forecastle gunmounting would have to be omitted. Subsequently two separate designs were produced in April 1940:

Type A: A ship with one set of twin torpedo tubes, and 4-4" guns on a waterline length of 272'.
Type B: A ship with one set of twin torpedo tubes, and 6-4" guns on a waterline length of 282'.

Eventually Design A was approved on 3.5.40 with the hull, general arrangements and machinery of the previous Type 2 vessels, except where modified by the torpedo requirements, but with one 4" gun mounting less. The dimensions of the ships remained the same and the weight of the Type 3 vessels was within 10 tons of the Type 2 vessels. However, it was necessary to fit 40 tons of permanent ballast. Vessels completed later had the stabilisers removed and the space utilised to carry 63 tons of extra fuel.

Thus the Type 3 vessels had the following characteristics:

Deep Displacement 1,545 tons.

Average speed on trials $26\frac{1}{2}$ knots at 375 rpm.

Maximum continuous speed of $25\frac{1}{2}$ knots, with a range of 1,050 miles.

The armament consisted of:

$4 \times 4''$ (2×2), one quadruple 2 pdr, 3 Single 20 mm guns.

1 twin — 21" torpedo tube/mounting.

Upon completion these vessels carried the Type 291 warning radar and the Type 285 fire control radar. Type 128 sonar was also carried.

Radar was fitted to earlier Type 1 vessels when they were refitted and Type 2 vessels had it fitted either on completion if available or during later refits.

BRECON AND BRISSENDEN (TYPE 4)

These two vessels were ordered under the 1940 War Emergency Programme on 27.7.40 from Thornycroft's. They differed considerably from the other Hunts and had an interesting design history.

The origin for the design went back to a proposal for a 1,000 ton destroyer made by Sir John Thornycroft to Sir Reginald Henderson, the Controller, in a letter of 24.10.38. Thornycroft proposed two designs — T/1267 and — T/1268 both with the same armament ($4 \times 4''$ and $2 \times 0.5''$ machine guns and quadruple torpedo tubes), but with speeds of 35 and 30 knots respectively.

The proposal was not acceptable to the DNC because:
1. He feared that the continuous casting over the boilers would fail as it had done with the leader GRENVILLE.
2. He did not like the idea of the forecastle deck (a strength deck) being opened for torpedo tubes.
3. The floodable length of the ship was greater than normal; the magazine stowage was too small; the low endurance; the absence of anti-submarine armament; the small wireless room; the crew would be too cramped, and the design had too large a silhouette.

The Thornycroft designs were not proceeded with and it was not until March 1940 after Admiral Bruce Fraser, the Third Sea Lord and Controller, had visited Thornycroft's that the proposals were revived.

Sir John Thornycroft in a letter to Sir Stanley Goodall, outlined the parameters for new designs based on the 1938 proposals. The designs (A to D) were for vessels of between 920 and 1,115 tons and between 260 ft and 280 ft in length with a speed in light condition of between 27 and $32\frac{1}{2}$ knots and armed with either two or three twin 4" guns, one quadruple two pounder pompom and two machine guns together with a complement of four depth charge throwers and 80 depth charges. A searchlight was to be carried.

These designs were again criticised by the DNC because:
1. No 2 mounting could not fire forward of 70° unless the two pounder crew evacuated their weapon.
2. The wireless office was too small.
3. The magazine and depth charge stores were too small.
4. It was anticipated that the ship would roll heavily.

In an attempt to meet the criticisms Thornycroft submitted a further three designs during 4.40:

T/1306   271' (oa) $\times$ 31$\frac{1}{2}$' (beam) $\times$ 15$\frac{1}{2}$' (depth), 1,000 tons (full load), with two twin 4" and one quadruple two pounder.

T/1307   260' (oa) $\times$31$\frac{1}{2}$' (beam) $\times$ 15$\frac{1}{2}$' (depth), 1,250 tons (full load) which omitted the searchlight but added three torpedo tubes.

T/1308   280' (oa) $\times$ 32$\frac{3}{4}$' (beam) $\times$ 15$\frac{1}{2}$' (depth), 1,475 tons (full load), 25,000 SHP 30$\frac{3}{4}$ knots and three twin 4" guns.   However, these further designs were criticised on the following grounds:
1. The discontinuity of strength due to the presence of the torpedo openings.
2. The restricted fuel tankage.
3. A likely propensity to roll quickly.

Following another meeting between Goodall and Fraser, Thornycroft's were invited to present a new general arrangement which took account of Admiralty criticisms.

This new design — T/1309P — was submitted by Thornycroft's on 31.5.40 and had the hull dimensions of: 280' (oa) $\times$ 35' $\times$ 16$\frac{1}{4}$' giving a full load displacement of 1,460 tons and a speed of 26$\frac{1}{2}$ knots. Subsequently the design T/1310 was submitted which included several improvements over previous designs:
1. The adoption of a continuous shelter deck.
2. A partially enclosed bridge.
3. Additional protective plating around the gun platforms.
4. A revised stern and keel line to improve the efficiency of the Asdics in bad weather.
5. An increase to 70 ft in the distance between the two pounder mounting and No 2 gun.
6. Quadruple torpedo tubes instead of a triple mounting.
7. A larger wireless office.

It was this design that was finally accepted, although on 8.8.40 the DNC specified triple torpedo tubes which were to be fitted on the weather deck with power training.

COMPARISONS BETWEEN THE ORIGINAL T/1310 DESIGN, THE DESIGN AS MODIFIED BY OCTOBER 1940 AND THE COMPLETED VESSEL

	T/1310 Design	Revised T/1310 (10.40)	As Completed
Length (waterline)	280'	283'	283'
Breadth (waterline)	33'	33¼'	33¼'
Standard displacement	1,140 tons	1,170 tons	1,175 tons
Shaft horsepower	19,500	19,500	19,000
Speed (Standard)	28 knots	28 knots	—
Speed (Deep)	26	—	25
Complement	170	—	167
Endurance at 20 knots	2,750 miles	2,350 miles	2,350 miles*
Endurance at 14 knots	4,400 miles	—	—
Armament	6 × 4"	6 × 4"	6 × 4"
	4 2 pdr	4 2 pdr	4 2 pdr
	2 Oerlikon	2 Oerlikon	4 Oerlikon
	2 Lewis	2 Lewis	2 Lewis
21" Torpedo Tubes	1 Quad	1 Triple	1 Triple
Depth Charge Throwers	2	2	4
Depth Charge Rails	—	—	2
Depth Charges	50	50	50
Fuel Oil	300 tons	285 tons	286 tons**
Full Load Displacement	1,480 tons	1,515 tons	1,561 tons

* In service 1,720 miles
** 352 in BRISSENDEN as stabilisers omitted.

A mock-up of BRISSENDEN's bridge structure during a wind tunnel test during 1941. Note that the wind is blowing directly from astern
(N.M.M.)

In December 1940, it was estimated that the Thornycroft Hunts would cost an additional £12,000 per hull over earlier Hunts as they were longer, had additional armament and the cost of the design had to be added as it had been prepared by the firm.

In the final design, the group weights of the vessels were:

Hull	655 tons
Machinery	305 tons
Armament	154 tons
Equipment	95 tons
Oil Fuel	286 tons
Reserve Feed Water	20 tons
Full Load Displacement	1,515 tons

Thus the two Type 4's were considerably superior to the first three Hunt types in that they were longer and more seaworthy because of the shelter deck. Also their armament was superior to the previous types as they had a six gun main armament and they carried torpedoes. Range and speed were similar to previous Hunts. Later, 55 tons of ballast was added, which contributed to a deep displacement of over 1,700 tons. Both vessels were highly successful in service, but it must be doubted if such a design should have been developed, when shipyard design capacity was stretched to the limit.

GROUP 5 HUNTS

During preliminary discussions on the 1941/42 Naval Building Programme in late 1940, 30 more Hunts were initially proposed for the Programme. The Naval Staff, however, preferred to order standard destroyers and the Hunts were deleted from the Programme. One cannot even say that these vessels reached the status of being projected.

THE 1942 PROPOSAL TO BUILD FURTHER HUNTS

On 13.9.42, in Minute M370/2, the Prime Minister asked:
   "Supposing you build nothing but Hunts and leave out the intermediates and the fleet types, how many more Hunts should we get at the expense of the larger kind?"
The Admiralty replied that without interfering with present production, 40 Hunts could be laid down before 12.43 with eight more being laid down each month after that time. Assuming 17 months for construction and adequate gun production, 11 Hunts could be completed in 1944, 75 in 1945 and 96 per year subsequently. Production of Fleet/Intermediate destroyers would be four per month, half the eventual rate of production of Hunts.
However, the Naval Staff, made the following additional points:
(1) We understand the need for a large number of escort vessels and have concentrated on the production of corvettes which are the most economical and easily produced type. These corvettes have the necessary endurance for crossing the Atlantic which the Hunts do not. Also, American production of escorts is increasing rapidly and she will help meet the need for escorts.
(2) The future needs of the Navy indicate a large carrier force augmented by battleships, cruisers and destroyers with a speed comparable with the heavy units, long endurance and excellent seaworthiness. The Hunts have a maximum speed of 26 knots, are of limited endurance and their size limits their ability to make headway in bad weather.
They concluded:
   "The Naval Staff is strongly opposed to the main units being hobbled by the inferior performance of the accompanying destroyers."
The matter was dropped.

THE PROPOSED ARMOURED HUNT

While the Type 4's were being discussed, Thornycroft's came up with a design (T/1312) for an Armoured Convoy Escort which was discussed with the DNC on 25.9.40. The objective of the design was to provide a "vessel of Hunt class dimensions and armament with such protection and sub-division as will enable it to withstand the effects of near misses and machine gun attacks". The armament was to be similar to that of Type 3 Hunts, but with machinery derated to 16,000 SHP. Standard displacement was to be 2,100 tons (2,440 tons deep), with a deep loaded speed of $21\frac{1}{2}$ knots. The dimensions of the proposed vessel were:
   Length (waterline) 295', breadth 41', draught (mean) $12\frac{1}{2}'$.
The vessel was to have a double bottom under the machinery spaces with an inner skin fore and aft. The hull was to be closely sub-divided to prevent undue listing if the side tanks were pierced. Finally some 500 tons of protection would be distributed over the machinery spaces where it was to be $2\frac{1}{2}''$. Side plating was to be covered with between $1\frac{1}{2}''$ and 2" of protection, as were the bridge, bridge front and wheelhouse. The DNC analysed the project and Mr Cole was damning in his report dated 3.10.40 on the design:
   "Thornycroft relies on the unprotected forecastle and poop to obtain his GZ and range, with a low GM. In a ship particularly designed to withstand near misses this is considered dangerous.Secondly, the drawing indicates that it is intended to secure the armoured plate on to the light structure by bolting or riveting. No attempt has been made to provide either transverse or longitudinal continuity of strength and on service the ship would probably break her back at the end of the gearing room."
No more was heard of the proposal!

THE HUNTS CONSTRUCTION DATES

1939 PROGRAMME

NAME	BUILDER	JOB NO	TEN ORDERED: 21.3.39 ALL TYPE 1's LAID DOWN	LAUNCHED	COMPLETED
ATHERSTONE	Cammell-Laird		8. 6.39	12.12.39	23. 3.40
BERKELEY	Cammell-Laird	J3302	8. 6.39	29. 1.40	6. 6.40
CATTISTOCK	Yarrow	J1834	9. 6.39	22. 2.40	22. 7.40
CLEVELAND	Yarrow	J1835	7. 7.39	24. 4.40	18. 9.40
EGLINTON	Vickers-Armstrong (Tyne): Parsons	J4091	8. 6.39	28.12.39	28. 8.40
EXMOOR (1)	Vickers-Armstrong (Tyne): Parsons	J4099	8. 6.39	25. 1.40	1.11.40
FERNIE	John Brown		8. 6.39	9. 1.40	29. 5.40

GARTH on the slip prior to launch 14.2.40   (Ian Buxton)

NAME	BUILDER	JOB NO	LAID DOWN	LAUNCHED	COMPLETED
GARTH	John Brown		8. 6.39	14. 2.40	1. 7.40
HAMBLEDON	Swan Hunter		8. 6.39	12.12.39	8. 6.40
HOLDERNESS	Swan Hunter		29. 6.39	8. 2.40	10. 8.40
	TEN ORDERED: 11.4.39		*ALL TYPE 1's*		
COTSWOLD	Yarrow	J1836	11.10.39	18. 7.40	16.11.40
COTTESMORE	Yarrow	J1837	12.12.39	5. 9.40	29.12.40
MEYNELL	Swan Hunter	J4114	10. 8.39	7. 6.40	30.12.40
MENDIP	Swan Hunter	J4111	10. 8.39	9. 4.40	12.10.40
PYTCHLEY	Scotts	J1111	26. 7.39	13. 2.40	23.10.40
QUANTOCK	Scotts	J1112	26. 7.39	22. 4.40	6. 2.41
QUORN	White	J6633	26. 7.39	27. 3.40	21. 9.40
SOUTHDOWN	White	J6602	22. 8.39	5. 7.40	8.11.40
TYNEDALE	Alex Stephen	J1471	27. 7.39	5. 6.40	2.12.40
WHADDON	Alex Stephen	J1472	27. 7.39	16. 7.40	28. 2.41

1939 WAR EMERGENCY PROGRAMME
17 ORDERED: 4.9.39   3 TYPE 1*   14 TYPE 2

NAME	BUILDER	JOB NO	LAID DOWN	LAUNCHED	COMPLETED
AVON VALE	John Brown	J1569	12. 2.40	23.10.40	17. 2.41
BLANKNEY	John Brown	J1570	17. 5.40	19.12.40	11. 4.41
BLENCATHRA*	Cammell-Laird	J3460	18.11.39	6. 8.40	14.12.40
BROCKLESBY*	Cammell-Laird	J3562	18.11.39	30. 9.40	9. 4.41
CHIDDINGFOLD	Scotts	J1115	1. 3.40	10. 3.41	16.10.41
COWDRAY	Scotts	J1116	30. 4.40	22. 7.41	29. 7.42
CROOME	Alex Stephen	J1477	7. 6.40	30. 1.41	29. 6.41
DULVERTON	Alex Stephen	J1478	16. 7.40	1. 4.41	27. 9.41
ERIDGE	Swan Hunter	J4129	21.11.39	20. 8.40	28. 2.41
HEYTHROP	Swan Hunter	J4139	18.12.39	20.10.40	21. 6.41
LAMERTON	Swan Hunter	J4142	10. 4.40	14.12.40	16. 8.41
KUJAWIAK (ex OAKLEY)	Vickers-Armstrong (Tyne): Parsons	J4145	22.11.39	30.10.40	17. 6.41
LIDDESDALE*	Vickers-Armstrong (Tyne): Parsons	J4136	22.11.39	19. 8.40	3. 3.41
KRAKOWIAK (ex SILVERTON)	White	J6583	5.12.39	4.12.40	28. 5.41
PUCKERIDGE	White	J6108	1. 1.40	6. 3.41	30. 7.41
WHEATLAND	Yarrow	J1849	30. 5.40	7. 6.41	3.11.41
WILTON	Yarrow	J1850	7. 6.40	17.10.41	18. 2.42

THREE ORDERED: 4 or 5.9.39   ALL TYPE 2

NAME	BUILDER	JOB NO	LAID DOWN	LAUNCHED	COMPLETED
LAUDERDALE	Thornycroft	J6153	12.12.39	5. 8.41	24.12.41
LEDBURY	Thornycroft	J6606	24. 1.40	27. 9.41	11. 2.42
FARNDALE	Swan Hunter	J4133	21.11.39	30. 9.40	27. 4.41

16 ORDERED: 20.12.39   ALL TYPE 2

NAME	BUILDER	JOB NO	LAID DOWN	LAUNCHED	COMPLETED
BADSWORTH	Cammell-Laird	J3260	15. 5.40	17. 3.41	18. 8.41
BEAUFORT	Cammell-Laird	J3560	17. 7.40	9. 6.41	3.11.41
SLAZAK/(BEDALE)	Hawthorn Leslie	J4202	25. 5.40	23. 7.41	9. 5.42
BICESTER	Hawthorn Leslie	J4210	29. 5.40	5. 9.41	18. 6.42
BLACKMORE	Alex Stephen	J1479	10. 2.41	2.12.41	14. 4.42
BRAMHAM	Alex Stephen	J1480	7. 4.41	29. 1.42	16. 6.42
CALPE	Swan Hunter	J4196	12. 6.40	28. 4.41	11.12.41
EXMOOR (II) (ex BURTON)	Swan Hunter	J4190	7. 6.40	12. 3.41	18.10.41
GROVE	Swan Hunter	J4199	28. 8.40	29. 5.41	5. 2.42
HURSLEY	Swan Hunter	J4139	21.12.40	25. 7.41	2. 4.42
HURWORTH	Vickers-Armstrong (Tyne): Parsons	J4207	10. 4.40	16. 4.41	5.10.41
MIDDLETON	Vickers-Armstrong (Tyne): Parsons	J4213	10. 4.40	12. 5.41	10. 1.42
OAKLEY (II) (ex TICKHAM)	Yarrow	J4145	19. 8.40	15. 1.42	7. 5.42
ZETLAND	Yarrow	J1854	2.10.40	6. 3.42	27. 6.42
SOUTHWOLD	J. S. White	J6274	18. 6.40	29. 5.41	9.10.41
TETCOTT	J. S. White	J6293	29. 7.40	12. 8.41	11.12.41

1940 WAR EMERGENCY PROGRAMME
SEVEN ORDERED: 4.7.40   ALL TYPE 3

NAME	BUILDER	JOB NO	LAID DOWN	LAUNCHED	COMPLETED
AIREDALE	John Brown	J1578	20.11.40	12. 8.41	8. 1.42
ALBRIGHTON	John Brown	J1579	30.12.40	11.10.41	22. 2.42
ALDENHAM	Cammell-Laird	J3766	22. 8.40	27. 8.41	5. 2.42
BELVOIR	Cammell-Laird	J3964	14.10.40	18.11.41	29. 3.42
CATTERICK	Vickers-Armstrong (Barrow)	J3886	1. 3.41	22.11.41	12. 6.42
DERWENT	Vickers-Armstrong (Barrow)	J3988	29.12.40	22. 8.41	24. 4.42
LIMBOURNE	Alex Stephen	J1490	8. 4.41	12. 5.42	24.10.42

ONE ORDERED: 19.7.40   A TYPE 3

NAME	BUILDER	JOB NO	LAID DOWN	LAUNCHED	COMPLETED
BLEASDALE	Vickers-Armstrong (Tyne): Parsons	J4283	31.10.40	23. 7.41	16. 4.42

NAME	BUILDER	JOB NO	LAID DOWN	LAUNCHED	COMPLETED
ONE ORDERED: AUGUST 1940 A TYPE 3					
ADRIAS (ex BORDER)	Swan Hunter	J4287	1. 5.41	3. 2.42	5. 8.42
SIX ORDERED: 28.7.40 4 TYPE 3, 2 TYPE 4*					
BLEAN	Hawthorn Leslie	J4247	22. 2.41	15. 1.42	23. 8.42
BRECON*	Thornycroft	J6069	27. 2.41	27. 6.42	18.12.42
BRISSENDEN*	Thornycroft	J6140	28. 2.41	15. 9.42	12. 2.43
PINDOS (ex BOLEBROKE)	Swan Hunter	J4284	3. 4.41	5.11.41	27. 6.42
EASTON	J. S. White	J6061	25. 3.41	11. 7.42	7.12.42
EGGESFORD	J. S. White	J6126	23. 6.41	12. 9.42	21. 1.43
15 ORDERED: 23.8.40 ALL TYPE 3					
ESKDALE	Cammell-Laird	J3269	18. 1.41	16. 3.42	31. 7.42
GLAISDALE	Cammell-Laird	J3369	4. 2.41	5. 1.42	12. 6.42
GOATHLAND	Fairfield	J1694	30. 1.41	3. 2.42	6.11.42
LA COMBATTANTE (ex HALDON)	Fairfield	J1695	16. 1.41	27. 4.42	30.12.42
HOLCOMBE	Alex Stephen	J1489	3. 4.41	14. 4.42	16. 9.42
MIAOULIS (ex MODBURY)	Swan Hunter	J4297	5. 8.41	13. 4.42	25.11.42
MELBREAK	Swan Hunter	J4293	23. 6.41	5. 3.42	10.10.42
KANARIS (ex HATHERLEIGH)	Vickers-Armstrong (Tyne): Parsons	J4295	12.12.40	18.12.41	10. 8.42
PENYLAN	Vickers-Armstrong (Barrow)	J3585	4. 6.41	17. 3.42	31. 8.42
ROCKWOOD	Vickers-Armstrong (Barrow)	J3989	29. 8.41	13. 6.42	4.11.42
HAYDON	Vickers-Armstrong (Tyne): Parsons	J4299	1. 5.41	2. 4.42	24.10.42
STEVENSTONE	J. S. White	J6056	2. 9.41	23.11.42	18. 3.43
TALYBONT	J. S. White	J6160	28.11.41	3. 2.43	19. 5.43
TANATSIDE	Yarrow	J1869	23. 6.41	30. 4.42	4. 9.42
WENSLEYDALE	Yarrow	J1870	28. 7.41	20. 6.42	30.10.42

Engines by builders except:

Vickers-Armstrong: built hulls at their Walker Yard on a sub contract basis for Parsons Marine Steam Turbine Co.

Wallsend Slipway and Engineering Co built engines for Swan Hunter & Wigham Richardson. They were a subsidiary of Swan Hunter.

THE BUILDING PROGRAMME OF THE HUNT CLASS

THE DATE	ORDERED				LAID DOWN				LAUNCHED				TOTAL BUILDING	COMMISSIONED				LOSSES	ACTUALLY IN SERVICE
	T1	T2	T3	T4	T1	T2	T3	T4	T1	T2	T3	T4		T1	T2	T3	T4		
31.3.39	10	—	—	—	—	—	—	—	—	—	—	—	10	—	—	—	—	—	—
30.6.39	11	—	—	—	9	—	—	—	—	—	—	—	20	—	—	—	—	—	—
3.9.39	2	—	—	—	18	—	—	—	—	—	—	—	20	—	—	—	—	—	—
30.9.39	5	17	—	—	18	—	—	—	—	—	—	—	40	—	—	—	—	—	—
31.12.39	—	27	—	—	20	6	—	—	3	—	—	—	56	—	—	—	—	—	—
31.3.40	—	23	—	—	12	10	—	—	10	—	—	—	55	1	—	—	—	—	1
30.6.40	—	9	—	—	8	24	—	—	11	—	—	—	52	4	—	—	—	—	4
30.9.40	—	4	27	2	—	27	1	—	13	2	—	—	76	10	—	—	—	—	10
31.12.40	—	2	21	2	—	23	7	—	4	8	—	—	67	19	—	—	—	—	19
31.3.41	—	1	16	—	—	19	12	2	1	12	—	—	63	22	1	—	—	1	22
30.6.41	—	—	5	—	—	12	23	2	—	13	—	—	55	23	8	—	—	1	30
30.9.41	—	—	1	—	—	5	23	2	—	16	4	—	51	23	12	—	—	1	34
31.12.41	—	—	—	—	—	—	19	2	—	12	9	—	42	23	21	—	—	1	43
31.3.42	—	—	—	—	—	—	12	2	—	8	12	—	34	23	25	4	—	3	49
30.6.42	—	—	—	—	—	—	4	1	—	1	15	1	22	23	32	9	—	6	58
30.9.42	—	—	—	—	—	—	2	—	—	—	10	2	14	23	33	16	—	8	64
31.12.42	—	—	—	—	—	—	1	—	—	—	2	1	4	23	33	25	1	10	72
31.3.43	—	—	—	—	—	—	—	—	—	—	1	—	1	23	33	27	2	11	74
30.6.43	—	—	—	—	—	—	—	—	—	—	—	—	—	23	33	28	2	12	74

THE LAUNCH OF BRISSENDEN 15.9.42
Top photo: Leaving the ways. Notice the pronounced knuckle in the bow *(N.M.M.)*
Bottom photo: Shortly after launch. The shelter deck is shown to advantage *(N.M.M.)*

DEPLOYMENT

By December 1940 17 Hunts had commissioned, of which CLEVELAND, TYNEDALE, FERNIE, BERKELEY, BLENCATHRA and ATHERSTONE were serving with the First Destroyer Flotilla at Portsmouth, whilst the remainder were stationed with the Nore Command. COTSWOLD, EGLINTON, EXMOOR (1), QUORN and SOUTHDOWN served with the 16th Flotilla at Harwich, whilst CATTISTOCK, GARTH, HOLDERNESS, PYTCHLEY, HAMBLEDON and MENDIP were in service with the 21st Flotilla at Sheerness, generally on convoy escort duties.

1941 was to see the first Hunt casualty, when EXMOOR (1) was lost off the east coast in February. However, by the end of the year, 42 Hunts had commissioned and they had become invaluable as replacements for the large numbers of fleet destroyers that had been lost. Additional flotillas had been formed or were forming at Plymouth, at Alexandra and attached to Force H consisting of a carrier, battleship and cruisers at Gibraltar.

In detail, the 41 vessels were allocated on 29.12.41 as follows:

At Scapa Flow	CALPE, CHIDDINGFOLD, PYTCHLEY (all working up)
On the Clyde	TETCOTT (refitting)
Rosyth Escort Force	LIDDESDALE, QUANTOCK, WHADDON
1st Flotilla (Portsmouth)	BERKELEY, BLENCATHRA, FERNIE, PUCKERIDGE, WHEATLAND
15th Flotilla (Plymouth)	BROCKLESBY, CLEVELAND, KRAKOWIAK (Pol), KUJAWIAK (Pol), TYNEDALE, ATHERSTONE (Refit)
16th Flotilla (Harwich)	COTSWOLD, EGLINTON, HAMBLEDON, SOUTHDOWN, QUORN.
21st Flotilla (Sheerness)	COTTESMORE, GARTH, HOLDERNESS, MENDIP, MEYNELL, CATTISTOCK.
At Southampton	LAUDERDALE (Unattached)
Force 'H' (Gibraltar)	CROOME, EXMOOR (II), BLANKNEY
2nd Flotilla (Alexandria)	AVON VALE, ERIDGE, FARNDALE, HEYTHROP
On passage to the Mediterranean via the Cape	BEAUFORT, HURWORTH (both at Freetown), SOUTHWOLD, DULVERTON (at Mombasa)

1942 was to see Hunt class destroyers engaged on fleet and escort duties in Home Waters, the Arctic and East Africa, but especially the Mediterranean, where seven of the class (SOUTHWOLD, HEYTHROP, GROVE, AIREDALE, KUJAWIAK, ERIDGE and BLEAN) were lost during the year, as were BERKELEY and PENYLAN in the Channel.

At the turn of the year, the number of completed units had reached 72. Operations were concentrated in the Western Mediterranean, following the 'Torch' operations. Attempts during the year to reinforce the East Indies Fleet had been thwarted by the demands of the Mediterranean Fleet and it was to be two years before any Hunts appeared in the eastern theatre of operations. At the end of 1942, the Hunts were deployed as follows:

At Scapa Flow:	
Attached to the Home Fleet:	BLANKNEY, BRECON, LEDBURY, MIDDLETON.
Working Up:	LA COMBATTANTE (Fr), EASTON, ADRIAS (Greek), MIAOULIS (Greek).
Rosyth Escort Force	BROCKLESBY, LIDDESDALE, WHADDON
1st Flotilla (Portsmouth)	ALBRIGHTON, BLEASDALE, GLAISDALE (Nor), ESKDALE (Nor).
15th Flotilla (Plymouth)	CLEVELAND, GOATHLAND, KRAKOWIAK (POL), LIMBOURNE, MELBREAK, SLAZAK (Pol), TANATSIDE, TYNEDALE, WENSLEYDALE.
16th Flotilla (Harwich)	SOUTHDOWN, ATHERSTONE, EGLINTON, HAMBLEDON, QUORN, COTSWOLD.
21st Flotilla (Sheerness)	BLENCATHRA, CATTISTOCK, COTTESMORE, FERNIE, GARTH, HOLDERNESS, MENDIP, MEYNELL, PYTCHLEY.
In the Mediterranean	
5th Flotilla	ALDENHAM, BEAUFORT, BELVOIR, CROOME, DERWENT, DULVERTON, EXMOOR, HAYDON, HOLCOMBE, HURSLEY, HURWORTH, ROCKWOOD, TETCOTT.
Not Allocated	PINDOS, KANARIS (both Greek).
57th Division	LAMERTON, WHEATLAND, WILTON.
58th Division	BICESTER, ZETLAND, BRAMHAM (damaged).
59th Division	AVON VALE, CALPE, FARNDALE, PUCKERIDGE.

With the Eastern Fleet at Kilindini:

        BLACKMORE, CATTERICK.

May 1943 was to see the peak strength of the Hunt class attained with 75 in commission, but by the end of the year this had been reduced to 66, by further heavy losses in the Mediterranean (DERWENT, PUCKERIDGE, HURWORTH, RHN ADRIAS (C.T.L.), DULVERTON, HOLCOMBE and TYNEDALE) and the loss of ESKDALE and LIMBOURNE in Home waters. Hunts chiefly undertook escort duties by this time, but were engaged on supply and patrol duties during the disastrous Aegean operations in the autumn of that year. The Hunts deployment on the last day of 1943 was as follows:

Home Fleet:	MIDDLETON (unallocated)
Rosyth Command	GOATHLAND
1st Flotilla	BLEASDALE, GLAISDALE (Nor), LA COMBATTANTE (Fr)
(Portsmouth)	STEVENSTONE, ALBRIGHTON.
15th Flotilla	BRISSENDEN, MELBREAK, TALYBONT, TANATSIDE,
(Plymouth)	WENSLEYDALE.
16th Flotilla	EGLINTON, SOUTHDOWN, COTSWOLD, QUORN (under repair)
(Harwich)	
21st Flotilla	CATTISTOCK, COTTESMORE, FERNIE, GARTH,
(Sheerness)	MEYNELL, PYTCHLEY, HOLDERNESS (under repair)
At Chatham	COWDRAY, AVON VALE (under repair)
At Liverpool	BADSWORTH (refitting)
Mediterranean:	
5th Flotilla	ALDENHAM, BEAUFORT, BELVOIR, RHN KANARIS,
(Algiers)	MIAOULIS, PINDOS.
22nd Flotilla	CROOME, EXMOOR, RHN THEMISTOCLES, RHN KRETI
(Algiers)	
58th Division	HAMBLEDON, BLENCATHRA, BLANKNEY, MENDIP, BRECON.
Mediterranean	ATHERSTONE, CALPE, CATTERICK, CLEVELAND, HAYDON,
Hunts (Malta)	FARNDALE, KRAKOWIAK (Pol), LIDDESDALE, SLAZAK (Pol).
Force 'K' Malta:	
57th Division	BROCKLESBY, LAMERTON, QUANTOCK, WHEATLAND,
	WILTON (repair)
59th Division	CHIDDINGFOLD, OAKLEY, BICESTER, ZETLAND.
60th Division	BLACKMORE, EGGESFORD, LAUDERDALE, LEDBURY,
	WHADDON.
Gibraltar	EASTON (under repair)

EASTON pictured off Gibraltar on 7.8.44 after undergoing repairs following her ramming of U458 off Sicily a year earlier
(N.H.B.)

1944 was to see the main theatre of naval operations return to Home Waters, with the build-up for the Normandy Landings and during the winter of 1944/45 the German inshore submarine campaign. A substantial number of vessels were still operating in the Mediterranean, but efforts were being made to reinforce the Eastern Fleet. The last vessel to be attached to the Home Fleet was withdrawn (MIDDLETON) and Hunts were now engaged purely on escort or patrol operations. 1944 saw GOATHLAND (C.T.L.) and QUORN lost in Home Waters whilst ALDENHAM became the final destroyer lost in the Mediterranean.

The Pink List of 29.12.44 showed the following dispositions.

At Hartlepool (Reserve)	GLAISDALE (Damaged)
15th Flotilla (Plymouth)	MELBREAK, BRISSENDEN, TANATSIDE.
16th Flotilla (Harwich)	ARENDAL (RNN Ex BADSWORTH), AVON VALE, COTSWOLD, EGLINTON, FARNDALE, HAMBLEDON, SLAZAK (Pol), KRAKOWIAK (Pol), STEVENSTONE (repair), TALYBONT (repair), SOUTHDOWN
21st Flotilla (Sheerness)	BLEASDALE, BRECON*, CATTISTOCK, COTTESMORE, COWDRAY, CROOME*, EGGESFORD, FERNIE, HAYDON, HOLDERNESS, LA COMBATTANTE (Fr), MENDIP, MIDDLETON, PYTCHLEY, BLANKNEY (Refit), GARTH (Repair), MEYNELL (Repair).
Former Combined Operations Vessel:	ALBRIGHTON
5th Flotilla (Alexandra)	LAMERTON, ATHERSTONE, BEAUFORT, CLEVELAND, LAUDERDALE, WHADDON, BELVOIR.
22nd Flotilla (Malta)	EXMOOR, CATTERICK, LEDBURY, LIDDESDALE, TETCOTT, WHEATLAND, CHIDDINGFOLD.
57th Destroyer Division (Malta)	QUANTOCK, BROCKLESBY, WILTON.
59th Destroyer Division (Malta)	*BICESTER, EASTON, OAKLEY, ZETLAND.
Aegean Escorts	KRITI, KANARIS, MIAOULIS, PINDOS, THEMISTOCLES (all Greek)

*Allocated to East Indies Fleet

To join Eastern Fleet (18th Flotilla)
BLACKMORE (at Sheerness)   CALPE (left Sheerness 28.12)

By 8.5.45 with the end of the European War, the last Hunt had been lost (LA COMBATTANTE) and the class had concentrated in the Nore Command with 38 vessels on station with the 16th and 21st Flotillas, 18 vessels were still in the Mediterranean and four on passage to the Indian Ocean.

The summer of 1945 saw a reduction in the number of Hunts on active service with the transfer of Greek and Norwegian vessels from Royal Navy operational control to their own service and the preparation of vessels for service against Japan. The number of Hunts in the East Indies grew as is shown in the Pink List of 3.9.45 when the class disposition was as follows:

Nore Command Local Escort:	GARTH, EGLINTON, HAMBLEDON, HOLDERNESS, MENDIP, KRAKOWIAK (POL), SLAZAK (POL).
Portsmouth Local Escorts:	COTTESMORE, CATTISTOCK, COTSWOLD.
Other Hunts in Service:	BROCKLESBY, QUANTOCK, SOUTHDOWN, BLENCATHRA FERNIE, PYTCHLEY, MEYNELL, BELVOIR.
Reserve Fleet:	GLAISDALE
At Rosyth for delivery to Norway:	ARENDAL
Refitting:	
UK:	ALBRIGHTON, BEAUFORT, EASTON, MELBREAK, WHEATLAND.
Mediterranean:	LEDBURY, TETCOTT, OAKLEY, TANATSIDE, TALYBONT, ZETLAND.
South Africa:	BLANKNEY, MIDDLETON, LAMERTON, WILTON, CATTERICK, LAUDERDALE.
Reserves for Eastern Fleet (In Mediterranean)	EXMOOR, HAYDON, CROOME, AVON VALE, STEVENSTONE, BRISSENDEN.
22nd Flotilla	LIDDESDALE, ATHERSTONE, CLEVELAND, WHADDON.
18th Flotilla (Trincomalee):	FARNDALE, BICESTER, BLACKMORE, BLEASDALE, BRECON, CHIDDINGFOLD.
On passage to 18th Flotilla:	COWDRAY, EGGESFORD.

ANALYSIS OF HUNT CLASS DESTROYERS LOST OR SERIOUSLY DAMAGED IN ACTION

Note: *Seriously damaged vessels are vessels out of action for over 3 months

Table 1

CAUSE	TOTAL LOSS	CONSTRUCTIVE TOTAL LOSS	SERIOUSLY* DAMAGED
1. AIR ATTACK (i) Bomb	HEYTHROP AIREDALE BERKELEY	—	FARNDALE BRAMHAM PUCKERIDGE ATHERSTONE BICESTER (By Own Forces) AVON VALE
(ii) Torpedo (iii) Glider Bomb	— DULVERTON	DERWENT ROCKWOOD	—
2. SURFACE ATTACK (ALL TORPEDO) (1) S-boat	PENYLAN ESKDALE (RNN)	—	—
(2) Torpedo Boat	LIMBOURNE	—	—
3. UNSPECIFIED EXPLOSION (MINE/TORPEDO)	EXMOOR (1) LA COMBATTANTE (Fr)	—	—
4. SUBMARINE ATTACK (ALL TORPEDO)	GROVE BLEAN PUCKERIDGE TYNEDALE HOLCOMBE	—	—
5. MINE	SOUTHWOLD KUJAWIAK (Polish) HURWORTH ALDENHAM	ADRIAS (Greek) GOATHLAND	BADSWORTH (Twice) COWDRAY COTSWOLD GLAISDALE HAMBLEDON HOLDERNESS PYTCHLEY QUORN STEVENSTONE
6. HUMAN TORPEDO/ EXPLOSIVE BOAT	QUORN	ERIDGE	BLENCATHRA
7. MARINE HAZARD	—	WENSLEYDALE (collision)	OAKLEY (hitting wreck)

COMMENTARY ON HUNT LOSSES

Almost half of the 86 vessels of the Hunt class received substantial damage or worse during their war service. This very fact is a strong indication of the strenuous service undertaken by vessels of the class.

The 43 major incidents, as shown in Table 1, can also be analysed further to show that the majority of casualties were caused by mines (16), closely followed by air attack (12), submarine attack (5), surface attack (3), explosive boats (3), unspecified explosions (2) and marine causes (2).

The danger to small vessels such as the Hunts when subject to torpedo attack is clearly illustrated by the fact that all eight vessels struck by the heavy torpedoes fired by submarines, torpedo boats and E-boats were lost. Some of the vessels such as the TYNEDALE sank very rapidly, with heavy casualties. Hunts stood a better chance against the lighter aerial torpedoes; both vessels which were struck by such devices, the DERWENT and AVON VALE, survived, although DERWENT had to be written off.

Again, the destructive effect of glider bombs on the Hunts that were unfortunately struck by such weapons was devastating, with the DULVERTON sinking and ROCKWOOD being declared a constructive total loss (C.T.L.).

However, the mine was the most serious hazard although not the most damaging to a small vessel such as a Hunt. Surviving a mine detonation was a matter of luck — depending on whether the destroyer's hull came into contact with the mine and on the damage control practised by the individual ship. Hunts could survive having their bows blown off, but any ship mined under the hull was especially vulnerable. Thus out of the ships mined ten survived, two were declared C.T.L. and the other four were lost.

Air attack was dangerous, especially the glider bombs as outlined above, but only three ships (HEYTHROP, AIREDALE and BERKELEY) were lost in bombing attacks and five others seriously damaged (including the BICESTER damaged by our own forces in 5.43 off Cape Bon). However, in the years 1941/2 when the Hunts were being used extensively as fleet destroyers and exposed to heavy air attack their strong AA armament protected them well.

Two vessels, EXMOOR and LA COMBATTANTE were lost by underwater explosion and in both cases there is some doubt as to whether the ships were mined or received torpedo damage. Only WENSLEYDALE was written off through collision and that was late in the war.

ERIDGE being towed into Alexandria by her sister ALDENHAM, after being immobilised off the Egyptian coast on 29.8.42. She was declared a constructive total loss and used as a base ship until scrapped in 1946. In the background is the French battleship LORRAINE demilitarised between 7.40 and 12.42

(Brownell Collection)

PROPOSED CONVERSION OF HUNTS TO A/S ESCORTS FOR THE POST WAR FLEET

By the end of the war the 55 Hunt class destroyers remaining in service with the Royal Navy had been rendered obsolete as the only alterations that had been undertaken during the war were:

1. The anti-aircraft armament of pompoms and Lewis guns had been supplemented as follows:
    Type 1 One quadruple pompom, one single pompom bow chaser
            Two Oerlikon. Two Lewis guns.
    Type 2 One quadruple pompom, one single pompom.
            Two twin Oerlikon. Some Type 2's had been fitted with 40 mm guns.
    Type 3 One quadruple pompom, three twin powered Oerlikons.
    Type 4 One quadruple pompom, four twin powered Oerlikons. Two Lewis guns.
2. Search and gunnery radars had either been fitted on refit during the war or for the later vessels on completion.

In a memo from the Director of Plans to the DNC on 26.3.46, proposals were made for the modernisation of the Hunts:

1. *ARMAMENT:*
    One twin 4" HA/LA.
    One Twin 40 mm STAAG with an outfit of two-thirds of normal supply of ammunition.
    One Single Bofors 40 mm Mk III mounting.
    Single Limbo A/S mortar with 20 salvoes or double Squid with 12 salvoes.
2. *EQUIPMENT:*
    Foxer/Unifoxer A/S equipment to be fitted.
    Radar to consist of the following types:
    Type 285 Air and Surface Warning
    Type 291 Air Warning
    Type 293 Surface/low-angle air search and target indication.
    VHF/Direction finding equipment to be fitted.
3. *OTHER MODIFICATIONS:*
    a. Forecastle and after deckhouse to be extended to improve habitability and provide space for radar offices.
    b. An enlarged bridge.
    c. Saving in top-weight by the use of aluminium alloy.
    d. Suppression of Mk V R/F director to save weight and because it would be extravagant with only one mounting and the fitting of a simpler type of fire control.
    e. Provision of additional dynamo power.

The deep displacement of the Types 2 and 3 Hunts by the end of the war had increased from 1,430 tons to 1,617 tons (including 40 tons of ballast) which would be raised on conversion (with 60 tons of ballast) to 1,636 tons.

A further Minute of 29.7.46 mentions that 8 × 60 kW dynamos were available from ERIDGE, DERWENT, ROCKWOOD and WENSLEYDALE, which had been scrapped. On 23.8.46 the last memo in the Cover suggested that two Hunts should be approved for conversion to prototype A/S vessels. Two 100 kW generators would replace the existing 60 kW generator. The increased weight of the Hunts since commissioning reduced the scope for increasing generator power so lightweight generators would need to be fitted.

No more is mentioned about this proposal and one can only assume that the idea was dropped because of the availability of larger and faster obsolete fleet destroyers, which had no stability problems and were more suitable for conversion. These fleet destroyer conversions were to join the fleet in the early 1950's as the Type 15 Full Conversion or the Type 16 Limited Conversion A/S frigates.

POST WAR SERVICE

The Hunts rapidly decommissioned and by December 1946 only ten were active — BRISSENDEN, HAYDON, STEVENSTONE and TALYBONT with the 3rd Destroyer Flotilla patrolling the Palestine Coast with the Mediterranean Fleet; BLEASDALE, COWDRAY, FARNDALE with the Nore Local Flotilla; BLENCATHRA and FERNIE utilised as air target vessels and EASTON a member of the third Escort Flotilla at Portsmouth. An eleventh vessel, BICESTER was refitting at Sheerness for service with the Nore Flotilla. The remaining vessels of the class, with the three exceptions mentioned below, never saw service with the Royal Navy post-war.

A year later only three vessels were on active service, with COWDRAY, BLEASDALE and BICESTER with the Nore Flotilla and the other vessels reducing to reserve. These three vessels were to serve with the Nore Flotilla until late 1950, when they also reduced to reserve. COWDRAY had rescued the few survivors from the submarine TRUCULENT which sank in the Thames in January 1950.

The other Hunts to see service post-war were WILTON which commissioned during 1949 as a member of the 4th Training Flotilla at Rosyth, but a year later was relegated to an Air Training Target Ship until 1952. MENDIP had been loaned to the Chinese Nationalists, but was returned to RN control on 29.5.49 and was used in the Far East until 12.9.49 covering the refit of the destroyer CONSORT. BROCKLESBY had been refitted at Devonport during 1951/2 as an experimental ship and was attached to the 2nd Training Squadron at Portland. Later on she was engaged solely on experimental anti-submarine duties, based at Portsmouth. She did not finally pay-off until 22.6.63, the last Hunt to see service with the Royal Navy.

A fine view of BICESTER as leader of the Nore Flotilla 10.48   *(N.M.M.)*

A REVIEW OF THE HUNT CLASS

The design was evolved very quickly in the year between the Munich crisis and the beginning of the war. The design was of necessity rushed and the mistakes made in the design gave the class initial stability problems. Although these were overcome, they meant that the class were weight critical throughout their careers. This factor led to their early demise from the fleet and to their relatively early disposal.

The importance of the Hunts was as a utility design which completed in large numbers at a time when the destroyer flotillas had suffered severe losses. They are important in that they filled the gap during 1941 and 1942 before the larger fleet destroyers entered service in quantity and after this time they formed an important element of the local escort flotillas especially in the Mediterranean and on the East Coast, where their low endurance and limited speed were not so important.

Captain T. D. Manning in 'The British Destroyer' wrote: "Their function was escorting, not fleet work, but they were tough little ships and very good indeed for their size. They were employed as convoy escorts on the East Coast, in the channel, in the Arctic and in the Mediterranean, but it was only the chronic shortage of larger escorts that caused them to be used on long trips such as the Russian convoys, for their endurance was limited and they had to refuel at sea too often, especially if they used high speeds which were often necessary on escort duty. They were not really up to fleet screening on account of their relatively low speed and small size, which cut them down in a seaway so it was hard to keep up without damage, but they were magnificent A/S ships, manoeuvrable, fast and with quick acceleration".

SHIP HISTORIES

An indistinct view of AIREDALE, but believed to be the only photograph of her in existence

(Maritime Photo Library)

AIREDALE (L07)

AIREDALE interrupted her work-up at Scapa to provide with MIDDLETON the AA escort for a portion of convoy PQ11's voyage to Iceland. AIREDALE was then allocated to the Mediterranean Fleet and sailed from the Clyde on 28.2.42 with the Corvette PETUNIA to escort the motor vessel QUEEN VICTORIA and the tug SALVONIA to Gibraltar. Following arrival at Gibraltar on 13.3.42 she sailed two days later to escort the cruiser DAUNTLESS to Simonstown, arriving on 3.4.42. She then joined the 5th Destroyer Flotilla at Alexandria on 1.5.42. She was soon in action when on 11.5.42 she joined DULVERTON and BEAUFORT in an unsuccessful attempt to tow the bomb-damaged destroyer JACKAL into Alexandria.

AIREDALE was lost on 15.6.42, barely six weeks after joining the 5th Flotilla, when escorting Convoy MWll to Malta, as part of the 'Vigorous' operation. She was set upon by 40 dive bombers south of Crete at position 33.50 N 23.50 E and was near-missed by two heavy bombs on her port side and one heavy bomb on her starboard side and received two bomb hits in the vicinity of her aft 4" mounting. A heavy explosion took place aft, with the 4" magazine and/or the depth charge magazine blowing up, and this started a serious fire in the after boiler room. The ship settled by the stern and was abandoned and was finally torpedoed by ALDENHAM. Nine officers and 124 ratings were rescued.

ALBRIGHTON (L12)

ALBRIGHTON suffered bomb damage at her builders at Clydebank so completion was delayed. Unusually she worked up at Greenock instead of Scapa before joining the First Destroyer Flotilla at Portsmouth during 4.42 after searching for ML443 missing from the St. Nazaire Raid of 28.3.42. ALBRIGHTON was to spend the next two years with this Flotilla on escort and patrol duties until her conversion to a Landing Ship Headquarters (Small) in the spring of 1944. She was to see action many times. On 24.4.42 she engaged a group of E-boats off Fécamp, damaging one; a fortnight later she engaged E-boats in the Channel and with SGBs 7 and 8 she intercepted a convoy off the Cotentin Peninsula on 19.6.42.

ALBRIGHTON received slight damage during the Dieppe Raid (19.8.42) when she had the melancholy task of sinking her sister BERKELEY previously damaged by air attack. Two months later in company with GLAISDALE, ESKDALE, COTTESMORE, FERNIE and QUORN she engaged the raider KOMET (Ship 14) and her escort. The KOMET was sunk during the action. ALBRIGHTON's only off-station employment during this time was to escort Convoy KMS2 (a 'Torch' convoy) with CLEVELAND and ESKDALE which arrived at Gibraltar on 9.11.42. The next day ALBRIGHTON escorted the torpedoed Dutch liner NIEUW ZEELAND into Gibraltar and a day later stood by the destroyer MARNE which had been badly damaged by torpedo. ALBRIGHTON

ALBRIGHTON in 3.43 when a member of the First Destroyer Flotilla based at Portsmouth   (N.H.B.)

returned to the UK on 18.11.42 as escort for Convoy MKF1 and resumed her normal duties. During the next 12 months, she was heavily engaged. With the destroyer WHITSHED, she attacked an enemy convoy off Dieppe on 11.12.42, she engaged a shore battery at Le Havre on 7.10.42, as well as sinking the Italian blockade runner BUTTERFLY during the night of 27-28.4.43 when she was seriously damaged with eight men killed and 25 wounded.

After her conversion, ALBRIGHTON controlled the landing of the reserve brigade on 'GOLD' Beach on 'D' Day and continued in this role for several weeks afterwards. She then reverted to patrol duties, attacking enemy trawlers on 12.8.44 and a fortnight later sank two trawlers 90 miles south of Lorient, rescuing 22 prisoners.

ALBRIGHTON converted back to a destroyer between 3.1 and 14.2.45, and then after working up, joined the 21st Destroyer Flotilla at Sheerness until the war's end. On 23.5.45 she was in collision with LST238 and her side was seriously buckled between frames 18 and 37. After repairs, she was allocated to the Eastern Fleet on 13.6.45 and refitted for this service at Immingham until 12.45. She then entered Category 'B' Reserve at Devonport on 8.1.46 remaining there until 1953. After a brief period at Penarth, ALBRIGHTON was towed to Gibraltar later in 1953 and she remained there in Class II Reserve until 1955. After a short period in Extended Reserve at Barrow, she was reduced to hulk status on 6.1.56.

ALBRIGHTON was one of seven frigates (with ACTAEON, FLAMINGO, HART, MERMAID, OAKLEY and EGGESFORD) earmarked on 3.5.56 for transfer to West Germany. She was finally sold on 11.11.57 and after a refit by Rutherford at Liverpool between 3.58 and 4.59, she commissioned in the West German Navy as RAULE on 14.5.59. She served for nine years as an anti-submarine training ship in the Baltic. RAULE decommissioned during 1968 and was sold for demolition the next year; finally being scrapped by Eisen & Metall, Hamburg.

ALDENHAM on 3.8.42. She is still not fitted with Type 271 radar. She was to become the last British destroyer lost in the Mediterranean when mined in the Adriatic on 14.12.44   *(I.W.M.)*

ALDENHAM (L22)

After working up at Scapa ALDENHAM joined the escort of Convoy WS17 on 20.3.42 and was soon in action: with GROVE, LEAMINGTON and VOLUNTEER she sank U587 in the North Atlantic on the 27th of the month. This was the first success of High Frequency Direction Finding (HF/DF) equipment. ALDENHAM, accompanied by GROVE, then rounded the Cape to join the 5th Destroyer Flotilla at Alexandria in 5.42. She was to remain in the eastern Mediterranean for the remainder of her career, from early 1943 becoming a member of the 22nd Flotilla. ALDENHAM undertook general patrol and escort duties in the Levant and participated in the unsuccessful 'Vigorous' convoy operation to Malta between 13-16.6.42. She undertook an anti E-boat sweep with DULVERTON, whilst the cruisers DIDO and EURYALUS bombarded Mersa Matruh on 20.7.42. A little over five weeks later, ALDENHAM towed the disabled ERIDGE into Alexandria following the bombardment at Daba.

The later months of 1942 and early 1943 were spent escorting replenishment convoys to Malta. This was followed by the blockade of Cape Bon in 5.43 and the escorting of convoys for the invasions of Sicily and Italy. ALDENHAM, like many of the class, was embroiled in the Aegean fiasco on supply and anti-shipping duties. She was lucky to survive undamaged, as she was near-missed by bombs on 14.11.43 and by a Hs293 glider bomb a week later. A further period of escort duties, punctuated by a short refit in Haifa in 4.44, preceded ALDENHAM's presence at the fourth major landing of the Mediterranean War — in the South of France between 9-14.8.44.

Her end came exactly four months later when at 1529 hours on 14.12.44 she struck a mine some 45 miles south-east of Pola. Five officers (including her CO) and 58 ratings were picked up by ATHERSTONE, but five officers and 121 ratings were lost.

ATHERSTONE (LO5)

ATHERSTONE was the only Type 1 vessel to ship the designed armament of six 4″ AA but when inclined in early 1940 she proved to be top-heavy and the modifications outlined earlier were effected. On completion she joined the First Destroyer Flotilla at Portsmouth on convoy duties in the Channel. On 11.9.40 she was damaged by two bombs and a near-miss whilst on escort duty in the Channel and was under repair at Chatham until 1.41 when she rejoined the First Flotilla until the end of that year.

In late 1941 ATHERSTONE joined the 15th Destroyer Flotilla at Plymouth and it was during this time that in company with CLEVELAND, BROCKLESBY and TYNEDALE, she escorted the raiding force for St. Nazaire during 27-28.3.42. Shortly afterwards she joined the 16th Destroyer Flotilla and escorted east coast convoys until 3.43 when she was one of the reinforcements sent to the Mediterranean for the invasions of Sicily and

Italy. ATHERSTONE stayed in the Mediterranean for the remainder of the war, participating in the invasion of the South of France in 8.44, whilst with the 18th Destroyer Flotilla. She joined the 5th Destroyer Flotilla at Alexandria in 11.44 until the end of the war.

ATHERSTONE in a sorry state whilst laid-up at Portsmouth in 1951   *(W.S.P.L. Kennedy)*

After spending the summer of 1945 in the Mediterranean, ATHERSTONE returned home and reduced to Category 'B' Reserve at Portsmouth in 10.45. She was never again active, being in Category 'B2' Reserve at Portsmouth until 1949, when she was downgraded to Category 'C'. In 1953 she was towed to Cardiff and reduced to Extended Reserve until 23.11.57 when she was handed over to the British Iron and Steel Corporation (BISCo) and towed to Port Glasgow for demolition by Smith & Houston, arriving there on 25.11.57.

AVON VALE (LO6)

After working-up, AVON VALE joined the Irish Sea Escort Force in 5.41, but was almost immediately loaned to the Mediterranean Fleet with seven other destroyers including ERIDGE and FARNDALE for a convoy operation to Malta, Operation 'Substance' in 7.41.

AVON VALE was then attached to the Mediterranean Fleet until 11.41 when she joined the Suez Escort Force, escorting convoys between Alexandria and Tobruk for three months. Whilst on these duties she picked up 20 ratings, the only survivors from the Australian sloop PARRAMATTA which had been torpedoed by U559 on 27.11.41.

In 2.42 she joined the 5th Destroyer Flotilla at Alexandria consisting of her sisters SOUTHWOLD, BEAUFORT, DULVERTON, HURWORTH, ERIDGE and HEYTHROP and during 2.42 escorted Convoy MW9A for Malta. She was then in action against the Italian Fleet at Sirte receiving damage by air attack and through collision on 22.3.42. On 29.3.42 AVON VALE left Malta as escort for the damaged cruiser AURORA (mined in 12.41), on passage to Gibraltar and the UK. Subsequently, she was under refit at Falmouth until 7.42. Then, after West African convoy duty between 9.42-10.42, she escorted convoys for the 'Torch' operations.

During 1.43 AVON VALE joined the 59th Destroyer Division of the Mediterranean Fleet and shortly afterwards, on 29.1.43, she was severely damaged by an aerial torpedo off the North African coast. The entire ship forward of the bridge front was blown away and the after end was towed to Gibraltar by BICESTER.

AVON VALE lay at Gibraltar for several months and made the passage to the UK under tow in convoy MKS15 between 25.6 and 4.7.43. It was not until 12.7.43 that permanent repairs were started at Chatham. After they had been completed, on 24.4.44, she undertook invasion escort duties until 7.44, when further repairs were undertaken on the Tyne. AVON VALE had been allocated to the Royal Hellenic Navy as AEGEAN in 3.44, but was not commissioned because of the mutinous condition of the Greek Navy at this time.

AVONVALE, on 19.5.44, shortly after being re-built at Chatham following torpedo damage off North Africa on 29.1.43 *(N.H.B.)*

Between 8 and 12.44, AVON VALE was a unit of the 22nd Destroyer Flotilla at Alexandria. She then returned to the UK. Previously, together with WHEATLAND, she sank the torpedo boat TA20 and the corvettes UJ202 and UJ208 west of Pag Island in the Adriatic at position 44.36 N 14.32 E on the night of 1-2.11.44. After a brief period in the UK, AVON VALE was refitted at Taranto before returning to the UK in 5.45 and was then prepared for service in the Far East.

The war being over, she was placed in Reserve on 9.12.45 and remained in Category 'B' Reserve at Devonport until 2.47, being then relegated to Category 'B2' until 1949. She was then refitted and laid up in Category 'A' Reserve at Sheerness, before being towed to Hartlepool and Supplementary Reserve. Finally, she was allocated to BISCo and scrapped at the Sunderland yard of T. Young on 15.5.58. Her scrap material realised a net total of £17,600.

BADSWORTH pictured here without Type 271 radar, survived two minings in the Mediterranean, but was out of service for nearly two years *(Brownell Collection)*

BADSWORTH (L03)/Norwegian ARENDAL

BADSWORTH was lucky to survive the war, as she suffered two minings and was out of service under repair for nearly two years of her career. Her first mining occurred off Grand Harbour, Malta on 16.6.42 when she was serving as part of the escort to the 'Harpoon' convoy to Malta. BADSWORTH sustained a hole 12' × 15' abreast the forward mounting and was flooded forward of No 1 4" magazine. After temporary repairs at Malta, in company with the destroyer MATCHLESS she acted as an escort for the empty transports ORARI and TROILUS which left Malta on 10.8.42. BADSWORTH was under repair on the Tyne until 11.42 when she rejoined the Londonderry Escort Force, with which she had served previously, including a Convoy (PQ15) to Murmansk from 20.4 to 5.5 and the returning QP12 from 21.5 to 29.5.42.

BADSWORTH joined the 60th Destroyer Division in 3.43 and was mined at the entrance to Bone harbour on 22.4.43. This second mining was far more serious and she had to be towed in by the minesweeper CLACTON. She suffered considerable hull damage under the quarterdeck with distortion from frames 120 to 150. The starboard main engine jammed and both shafts were distorted.

Following temporary repairs at Malta, BADSWORTH was towed to the UK by the tug FRISKY as part of Convoy MKS15 and was under repair at Liverpool until 11.44. Whilst completing her repairs, BADSWORTH was transferred on loan to the Royal Norwegian Navy on 9.8.44 as ARENDAL and served with the 16th Destroyer Flotilla at Harwich until the war ended. On the night of 25-26.3.45 with KRAKOWIAK and the frigate RIOU she drove off E-boats of the 4th and 6th Flotillas which had been laying mines in the Thames Estuary.

On 8.6.45 BADSWORTH's permanent sale to Norway was confirmed and after being re-rated as a frigate in 1956, she was stricken on 1.5.61.

ARENDAL in 1952. She has changed very little since 1945 *(W.S.P.L. Kennedy)*

A war view of BEAUFORT. In 7.53 she was transferred to Norway as HAUGESUND and was not stricken from service until 1965 *(Brownell Collection)*

BEAUFORT (L14)

After completion, BEAUFORT rounded the Cape with Convoy WS14 and joined the 5th Destroyer Flotilla at Alexandria in 2.42, serving with this flotilla for the whole of her war career. She saw much action being engaged at the Battles of Sirte in 2.42 and 3.42, whilst covering Malta Convoys and in 6.42 was an escort for the 'Vigorous' convoy. Later in the war, she saw service at the landing in Sicily, Salerno and during the abortive Aegean Campaign of 10-11.43. She then saw further action at the Anzio Landings (21.1.44) and finally during the South of France Landings in 8.44.

BEAUFORT returned to the UK at the end of the war and refitted at Cardiff between 10.6.45 and 24.9.45 but was relegated to Reserve at Devonport on 8.12.45, remaining there until 1952. (Category 'B2' 1947-1.49 and then Category 'C'). On 31.10.51 with her sister ZETLAND she was loaned to the Royal Norwegian Navy free of charge for four years. After being refitted by Messrs T. R. Dowson on the Tyne, she was renamed HAUGESUND on 13.7.53 and transferred to the Norwegians at Newcastle on 30.9.54. In 1956 she was sold outright to the Norwegian Navy and served another nine years until stricken in 1965.

BEDALE as the Polish SLAZAK. She saw no active service with the Royal Navy. Transferred to India post-war, she survived until 1979
(N.H.B.)

BEDALE/Polish SLAZAK (L26)

BEDALE never saw active service with the Royal Navy, because under the Anglo-Polish Naval Agreement of 19.2.42, she was turned over to the Polish Navy and commissioned at SLAZAK. The 15th Destroyer Flotilla at Plymouth was SLAZAK's unit until she had to undergo weather damage repairs at Liverpool in 2.43. Earlier SLAZAK had been an escort at the Dieppe raid of 19.8.42, where she had received minor damage. SLAZAK was one of the reinforcements for the Mediterranean Fleet during 6.43.

SLAZAK was to spend ten months in the Mediterranean, first with the Gibraltar Escort Force (6.43-8.43), then the 59th Destroyer Division (8.43), followed by the 48th Escort Group (9.43-12.43), then with Mediterranean Hunts (12.43-3.44) and finally the 18th Destroyer Flotilla for her final month in the Mediterranean.

After further escort duties with the 15th Destroyer Flotilla from 4.44 to 10.44 in support of the Normandy invasion, she joined the 16th Destroyer Flotilla at the Nore until the end of the war. SLAZAK remained an active member of the Nore Flotilla until her loan period with the Poles was terminated on 23.7.46 at which time she reverted to her old name of BEDALE. As BEDALE, she was to remain in reserve at Harwich from 28.9.46 until 1952 (in Category B1 to 15.2.47, Category B2 to 1949 and then Category B).

On 17.6.52, it was announced that she was to be loaned to the Indian Navy for three years after being refitted by Cammell-Laird's at Indian expense. She was renamed GODAVARI on 27.11.52 and commissioned into Indian service on 27.4.53, serving as a training vessel until stricken in 1979. In the meantime, she was sold outright to India in 4.59.

BELVOIR (L32)

BELVOIR was very active throughout her career, her duties commencing whilst working up in 4.42 when she escorted the Battleship KING GEORGE V which was covering Convoys PQ15/QP11. She left the UK on 10.5.42, escorting Convoy WS19 to Capetown and reached Durban on 15.6.42 to refuel with her sister HURSLEY. She was then detached to escort the Armed Merchant Cruiser MORETON BAY to Kilindini arriving there on 8.7.42. Although she was originally intended to serve with the 2nd Flotilla of the Eastern Fleet, BELVOIR was loaned to the Mediterranean Fleet in 6.42 and never returned.

She joined the 5th Destroyer Flotilla on 17.8.42 but before this she had escorted the cruiser DIDO during the bombardment of Mersa Matruh on 23.7.4 and two days later escorted the damaged submarine PORPOISE to Port Said. On 14.9.42 BELVOIR left Alexandria in company with ALDENHAM to escort the tug BRIGAND while the latter endeavoured to tow the damaged cruiser COVENTRY and the destroyer ZULU into Alexandria. However this was to no avail as both vessels had already sunk.

In 10.42, BELVOIR undertook two feint operations in support of the general attack at Alamein and shortly afterwards was engaged in regular convoys to supply Malta between 11.42 and 2.43. She was an escort for Operation 'Stoneage' during 11.42 and the subsequent Convoys MW14, ME11, MW16, ME12, MW20B and ME17.

BELVOIR. Note that the searchlight is present and there are no radars   *(N.H.B.)*

On the 1.2.43 BELVOIR and TETCOTT picked up the CO, five officers and 112 ratings from the minelayer WELSHMAN which had been torpedoed at 0145 hours at position 32.12 N 24.52 E off the Egyptian coast. The rest of 1943 was spent on invasion duties at Sicily and Salerno, and during 10-11.43 on operations in the Aegean. On 30.10.43 she was hit by a bomb which did not explode, but did, however, penetrate the stabiliser compartment. The bomb was removed and thrown overboard. Two weeks later, on 13.11.43 BELVOIR and ECHO picked up six officers and 103 ratings from the DULVERTON when she was lost to glider bomb attack.

BELVOIR was offered on loan to the French Navy on 15.6.44 but this offer was not accepted. She remained in the Mediterranean, except for a brief period supporting Normandy convoys and took part in indecisive engagements with German torpedo boats on 20.9.44 off the Albanian coast and a U-boat on 4.10.44 at 40.38 N 13.21 E. BELVOIR returned to the UK in 7.45 and reduced to Category 'B' reserve at Portsmouth. She never re-entered service, being in reserve until 1957. She was in Category 'B' at Portsmouth until 1950, then at Harwich until 1952, but returned to Portsmouth from 1952 until 1955 when she entered Extended Reserve, still at Portsmouth, until her disposal. BELVOIR arrived for demolition at the Bo'ness yard of P & W MacLellan Ltd on 21.10.57.

BERKELEY. This view taken shortly after commissioning in 6.40 gives a good view of the false bow wave, the plastic armour around the bridge and the complete absence of radar   *(Brownell Collection)*

BERKELEY (L17)

In 6.40, whilst officially working up before joining the First Destroyer Flotilla at Portsmouth, BERKELEY escorted convoys of evacuated allied troops from ports in the west of France to the UK, unsuccessfully attacking a U-boat on 7.6.40. Subsequently, for the remainder of her career with the First Flotilla she escorted convoys in the Channel and North Sea. She was slightly damaged by the explosion of a mine 30 yards off her port quarter on 20.12.40, in the outer Medway Bar which entailed six days repairs. In addition, BERKELEY was engaged in one of the unsuccessful attempts to intercept the German battlecruisers during the 'Channel Dash' on 15.2.42.

She was lost by air attack off Dieppe on 19.8.42, when one of several Hunts (including CALPE, GARTH, ALBRIGHTON, BLEASDALE, BROCKLESBY, SLAZAK and FERNIE) escorting the raiding force to Dieppe. BERKELEY received two direct hits on the starboard side on the upper deck forward of the bridge. Her back was broken and her fore-end flooded. She was abandoned with a heavy list to starboard and down in the bows and was finally dispatched by a torpedo from ALBRIGHTON.

BICESTER pictured at the Coronation Review in 7.53 as a representative of the Reserve Fleet. Note that all the gun mounts and radars are cocooned
(W.S.P.L.)

BICESTER (L84)

Immediately following her commissioning on 18.6.42, BICESTER joined the Londonderry Special Escort Division until 11.42, when she joined the 58th Destroyer Division at Algiers until 5.43. Whilst based at Londonderry in 8.42 she formed part of the escort for the 'Pedestal' Convoy to Malta. She was detached from the convoy with her sisters DERWENT and WILTON as escort for the cruiser NIGERIA that had previously been torpedoed. This was followed by escort duties to Iceland, and later she supported the landing at Oran in 11.42.

On 23.2.43, in company with LAMERTON, WHEATLAND and WILTON, she sank U443 west of Algiers. Her service in the Mediterranean was curtailed on 9.5.43, for when engaged in blockading operations off Cape Bon, she was attacked and badly damaged by the fire from 18 Spitfires. One bomb exploded underneath her and she was flooded between bulkheads 134 and 108. After temporary repairs at Malta, permanent repairs were undertaken in the UK and completed in 10.43.

BICESTER then joined the 59th Destroyer Division at Malta, where she served until the end of the war. However, whilst at Bari on 2.12.43, she and her sister ZETLAND received considerable damage, when the port was bombed and an ammunition ship exploded near them. BICESTER was towed to Taranto, by ZETLAND and was under repair until 15.1.44.

She spent the next six months escorting convoys and undertaking patrols in the Adriatic and Tyrrhenian Seas, before acting as an escort for the South of France invasion of 8.44. Her final months of Mediterranean service were spent in the Aegean and she acted as guardship at Piraeus from 11.44 until 2.45, when she arrived to refit at Alexandria. Following her return to the UK in 5.45 for tropicalisation modifications, she went east in 7.45 and became leader of the 29th Destroyer Flotilla at Bombay.

BICESTER returned to Sheerness on 4.12.45 and immediately joined the Nore Flotilla (acting as leader from 7.47) until 1.50 when she paid off into Category 'A' Reserve at Chatham until 1955. In 7.53 she was one of the representatives of the Reserve Fleet at the Coronation Review. In 1955/56 she was in Extended Reserve at Chatham. She arrived at T. W. Ward's yard at Grays, Essex on 23.8.56 for demolition.

BLACKMORE pictured on 15.1.45 on completion of her refit at Sheerness prior to further service in the Indian Ocean
(N.H.B.)

BLACKMORE (L43)

BLACKMORE had probably the widest range of service of any Hunt after her completion on 14.4.42. After work-up, she escorted convoy WS20 to the Cape, before undertaking escort duties with the 2nd Destroyer Flotilla, east of the Cape of Good Hope. After refitting at Simonstown between 3-5.43, BLACKMORE spent three months with the West African Command and then joined the Mediterranean Fleet in 8.43 for fourteen months.

In the Mediterranean, she was a unit of the 57th Destroyer Division. She then joined the 20th Destroyer Division in 11.43 and from 6.44, the 5th Destroyer Flotilla. On the night of 11-12.6.44 she and EGGESFORD encountered four E-boats off the Jugoslav coast. These were put to flight and ten prisoners were taken from the E-boat that was sunk.

BLACKMORE returned to the UK and refitted at Sheerness between 10.44 and 2.45. After a brief period attached to Nore Command, she arrived at Bombay on 28.3.45 for service with the 18th Destroyer Flotilla at Trincomalee. She acted as a weather ship for the invasion of Rangoon in 5.45.

She left Singapore on 8.10.45 for the UK, arriving at Devonport in 12.45 and was immediately paid off into Category 'B' Reserve. She remained in reserve (Category 'B2' after 15.2.47 and Category 'C' by 6.49) until formally accepted on loan by the Royal Danish Navy on 18.7.52. On 28.2.53, she was renamed ESBERN SNARE on commissioning with the Danes and served with them until stricken in 1966 after her loan period had been renewed.

ESBERN SNARE in 1959. Note the new lattice mast, 40mm guns and improved radar fit
(W.S.P.L. Kennedy)

BLANKNEY pictured during 6.43 prior to her transfer to the Mediterranean. The lantern of her Type 271 radar is shown clearly as is the camouflage pattern   *(N.H.B.)*

BLANKNEY (L30)

BLANKNEY was very active, especially in her first two years of service. After working up, she joined the Irish Sea Escort Force until 11.41, then, after a brief period with the 12th Escort Group, she joined the 20th Escort Group at Londonderry in 12.41. However, her period of service with the Group was to be short, because after carrying RAF stores to Gibraltar in company with the destroyer ARROW, she was attached to the 13th Destroyer Flotilla based at Gibraltar and supported the 'HG' Convoys between Gibraltar and the UK.

In 12.41 she participated in the sinking of U131 on the 17th and rammed and sank the U434 the next day whilst escorting HG 76 to Gibraltar. BLANKNEY suffered as a result of this ramming and was under repair at Gibraltar until 9.2.42. She was immediately back in action as an escort with the 37th Destroyer Division with Force 'H' during Operations 'Spotter' between 6-8.3.42 and 'Picket' between 20.3.-30.3.42. 'Spotter' and 'Picket' were both flying-off operations for aircraft to Malta.

BLANKNEY returned to the UK in 4.42 and operated with the 6th Destroyer Flotilla of the Home Fleet for the next thirteen months, except whilst being refitted on the Humber between 29.9.-16.11.42. In addition to the usual escort duties BLANKNEY escorted the battleship KING GEORGE V back to the UK in 5.42 after she had been damaged in a collision with the destroyer PUNJABI. She also escorted the Convoy PQ16 to Russia from 16.5.42 and with BADSWORTH, KUJAWIAK and MIDDLETON, was part of the escort for the 'Harpoon' Malta convoy a month later. BLANKNEY was also an escort for the covering force of the ill-fated PQ17 convoy and with the destroyers MIDDLETON, MARNE and MARTIN sailed with ammunition for Murmansk arriving on 24.7.42.

Whilst at Archangel on 30.7.42, BLANKNEY was involved in a collision which necessitated her remaining there until 12.9.42. Subsequently, she escorted convoys PQ18 and QP14 to and from Russia during 9.42.

In 7.43, after escorting Convoy KMF17 to the Mediterranean, BLANKNEY served as an escort for Operations 'Husky' and 'Avalanche'. During this time her primary duties with the 58th Destroyer Division were as an escort vessel. However, on 13.7.43 she was in collision with BRISSENDEN, which received serious damage. On 8.3.44 she was one of an allied squadron which sank U450 south of Anzio. Later, a few days before her departure for the UK to participate in the Normandy landings, she was one of the vessels to sink U371 off Gibraltar on 4.5.44. Her Normandy escort duties were as an unattached vessel based at Portsmouth. These were completed in 9.44 when she joined the Dover Patrol for two months until her refit at Liverpool between 11.44 and 6.1.45. She spent the last months of the war with the 21st Destroyer Flotilla at Sheerness containing the German inshore submarine campaign.

On 14.7.45 BLANKNEY sailed from Plymouth for the Cape, and refitted at Simonstown until 7.12.45 when she set off to return to the UK, reducing to reserve at Devonport on 14.5.46. BLANKNEY was to remain in reserve until she was approved for scrapping on 22.10.58. She remained in Category 'B' Reserve until 2.47 and then Category 'B2' until refitted in 9.48. She then transferred to Category 'A1' Reserve at Sheerness for the next four years being then transferred to Category II Reserve at Hartlepool until her disposal. BLANKNEY arrived at Blyth on 7.3.59 for scrapping by Hughes Bolckow. Demolition was completed by 27.7.59.

BLEAN is seen here a month after commissioning in 8.42. Notice she still carries her searchlight and it is unlikely that she was altered before her loss three months later   *(N.H.B.)*

BLEAN (L47)
BLEAN had the shortest career of any of the Hunts. After her work-up at Scapa, followed by some repairs on the Thames, BLEAN escorted a convoy to Gibraltar arriving there on 2.11.42. The whole of her active service then was with the 58th Destroyer Division, based at Algiers, escorting 'Torch' convoys. On 11.12.42, whilst escorting convoy MKF4 some 60 miles west of Oran, she was torpedoed by U443. The destroyer WISHART reported that the first torpedo hit aft on the starboard side. The second torpedo struck forward on the starboard side. The BLEAN was enveloped in a pall of smoke and rolled over onto her starboard side and sank by the stern, four minutes after the first torpedo hit. Eight officers and 86 ratings were picked up, but 89 ratings were lost.

BLEASDALE (L50)
BLEASDALE stayed in Home Waters for the whole of the European War, serving with the First Destroyer Flotilla at Portsmouth until 10.44, when she transferred to the 21st Destroyer Flotilla at Sheerness for the remainder of hostilities. Her only excursion into warmer waters was to escort a 'Torch' Convoy to Gibraltar between 30.11.42 and 8.12.42.

Subsequently, BLEASDALE served as a convoy escort on patrol and anti E-boat duties in the Channel, having been an escort for the Dieppe Landings on 19.8.42 when she sustained minor damage. On 10.10.42 she received mine damage off the Nab Tower, which necessitated a month's repair at Portsmouth.

After refitting at Sheerness between 2 and 4.45 and receiving modifications on the Thames for Eastern service, BLEASDALE worked up in the Mediterranean and joined the 18th Destroyer Flotilla at Trincomalee in 8.45, being present at the re-occupation of Port Swettenham in 9.45. BLEASDALE quickly returned to the UK and paid off into reserve at Chatham on 26.11.45. However, she soon recommissioned in 2.46, for one of the longest periods of activity of any Hunt post-war, with the Nore Local Squadron. On 18.4.47 she acted as firing ship for the radio activated demolition charges which destroyed the fortifications on Heligoland.

BLEASDALE entered Category 'A' Reserve at Sheerness on 21.4.52, but soon transferred to Portsmouth to refit, before entering Category I Reserve for the next year. She was in lowering categories of reserve (Category II 1953/4, Category III from 1954) until 12.9.56 when it was announced that she had been transferred to BISCo and allocated to Hughes Bolckow, arriving at Blyth on 14.9.56. Demolition was completed by 28.1.57.

This wartime view of BLEASDALE, shows clearly the 2pdr bow-chaser, which was widely fitted to Hunts that saw service on the east coast   *(Brownell Collection)*

This second view of BLEASDALE, on 27.2.52, prior to entering reserve after one of the longest periods of post war active service of any Hunt. She had served with the Nore Local Squadron   *(N.M.M.)*

BLENCATHRA (L24)

After a short work-up BLENCATHRA joined the First Destroyer Flotilla at Portsmouth on escort and patrol duties until late 1942. During this period BLENCATHRA sustained minor action damage on 14.3.42 and again on 18.7.42 when she was near-missed in the Channel and damaged by aircraft cannon fire. On the night of 28-29.3.42 while escorting Convoy FS1074, she engaged units of the German 2nd MTB. Flotilla off Smiths Knoll. BLENCATHRA then joined the 21st Flotilla at Sheerness and spent the ensuing months on east coast convoy escort duties.

BLENCATHRA laid up with a sister at Barrow on 21.5.56   (Ken Royall)

BLENCATHRA was then transferred to the 58th Destroyer Division of the Mediterranean Fleet in 7.43 in time to participate in the Sicily landings. Although primarily engaged on escort duties, she took part in the Aegean Campaign in the autumn of 1943 and shelled Leros with the destroyers PENN and ALDENHAM on the night of 14-15.11.43. The highlights of her Mediterranean service were her participation with EXMOOR (II), BLANKNEY and BRECON in the sinking of U450 off Anzio on 10.3.44, and U223 on 29.3.44.

BLENCATHRA was recalled for invasion service at Normandy as an unattached vessel. On 3.8.44, whilst hoisting aboard a human torpedo, she was slightly damaged when the torpedo's scuttling charge blew up. This period of duty off Normandy was followed by further service on escort duties with the 21st Flotilla of the Nore Command until the war's end.

After being damaged in collision with SS WILLOWDALE on 15.8.45, BLENCATHRA's armament was removed between 16.10.45 and 21.10.45 during conversion into an Aircraft Target Ship at Rosyth. She remained on these mundane but necessary duties, until reduced to Category B2 reserve on 19.7.48.

On 16.1.50, BLENCATHRA and CATTISTOCK were offered on loan to Norway, but the proposed loan was cancelled three months later on 15.4.50 and two Type 2's substituted. BLENCATHRA spent the rest of her career in reserve, first in Category 'C' at Harwich between 1949 and 1953 and then in Extended Reserve at Barrow until 1957. On 11.10.56 it was announced that BLENCATHRA with her sisters ATHERSTONE, CATTISTOCK, CROOME, CLEVELAND, FERNIE, HOLDERNESS, MELBREAK, PYTCHLEY and SOUTHDOWN had been approved for scrap. BLENCATHRA remained at Barrow and was handed over to T. W. Ward Ltd on 2.1.57 who carried out her demolition there. A letter from BISCo of 4.2.58 confirmed that demolition had been completed.

BORDER/Greek ADRIAS (I) (L67)
Launched on 3.2.42 as BORDER, she was renamed ADRIAS, before completion, on her transfer to the Royal Hellenic Navy on 16.5.42.

The work-up of ADRIAS was delayed by damage she received at Scapa in 8.42, and this necessitated repairs at Wallsend until 12.42. After a further work-up period at Scapa, ADRIAS formed part of the escort of Convoy WS26 to Freetown during January 43. After circumnavigating Africa, she joined the 22nd Destroyer Flotilla at Alexandria until her loss.

ADRIAS (ex BORDER) on completion on 31.7.42. Note that she still mounts a searchlight   *(N.H.B.)*

ADRIAS is best remembered for her epic journey from the Aegean to Alexandria after being seriously damaged by a mine east of Calino Island on 22.10.43 during the ill-fated Aegean campaign. The whole of her bow forward of frame 37 completely disappeared, whilst her forward 4" gun was damaged beyond repair, as were her radars, asdic, bridge electrics and high power and low power switch-boards, but her main and auxiliary machinery escaped damage. She was towed into Turkish territorial waters and emergency repairs undertaken at Gumusluk. She was escorted by the MTBs 645, 646 and 647 to Kakava Bay off Casteloriso, where she arrived on 3.12.43. Here she was joined by the destroyers JERVIS and PENN as escort for the tug BRIGAND. She was towed by BRIGAND to Limassol under heavy air attack. After a day at Limassol, ADRIAS proceeded under her own power, since towing had been found to be unsatisfactory due to excessive yaw and she finally arrived at Alexandria on 6.12.43, a passage of 600 miles with her bows blown off.

She was declared a constructive total loss and was initially laid-up at Alexandria and then Newcastle-upon-Tyne after 12.44. On 7.10.45 it was announced that ADRIAS was to be scrapped and she arrived at the Gateshead yard of Messrs King & Co on 20.11.45 for demolition.

BRAMHAM/Greek THEMISTOCLES (L51)

After working up, BRAMHAM joined the Londonderry Special Escort Division in 8.42 and immediately formed part of the escort for the 'Pedestal' Convoy to Malta with DERWENT, BICESTER and LEDBURY. BRAMHAM escorted the damaged transport DEUCALION (until lost) and later with PENN and LEDBURY escorted the tanker OHIO into Malta on 13.8.42. BRAMHAM returned to the UK as escort for the damaged aircraft carrier INDOMITABLE and immediately left for Scapa where she acted as an escort for oilers to Iceland during the PQ18/QP14 operation of 9.42.

On 20.10.42 she left Londonderry with BLYSKAWICA and COWDRAY for Gibraltar on escort duties in connection with the 'Torch' operation. Whilst on these duties on 20.11.42 between Phillipeville and Bougie BRAMHAM was hit by a bomb on the upperdeck aft abreast the 4" gun-mounting. The bomb penetrated the ship and exploded in the sea beneath her. She received much structural damage and was flooded. After temporary repairs at Algiers, BRAMHAM left on 20.12.42 for Gibraltar where further repairs were undertaken until 24.1.43 when she sailed for the UK as additional escort for MK56. She was under repair on the Tyne between 9.2.43 and 10.7.43. Meantime, she was handed over to the Royal Hellenic Navy in 2.43 and renamed THEMISTOCLES.

41

BRAMHAM shortly after commissioning in 8.42. Six months later she was transferred to the Royal Hellenic Navy as THEMISTOCLES and served them until 1960 *(N.H.B.)*

THEMISTOCLES arrived back on the Levant Station on 30.9.43 and was immediately embroiled in the Aegean Campaign for the next two months before undertaking more normal escort duties for the rest of her service. She was however involved in the Anzio Landings (1.44), the South of France Landings (8.44) and the re-occupation of the Aegean Islands in 10.44. By the end of 1944, THEMISTOCLES was a unit of the 12th (Greek) Flotilla at Piraeus and served with the Greek Navy until 12.12.59 when she was returned to the Royal Navy in Greece and sold to Greek shipbreakers on 30.6.1960.

This fine view of BRECON taken on 18.12.42 whilst on trials. The picture gives a good indication of how different the two Type 4's were compared with the remainder of the class *(N.M.M.)*

BRECON (L76)

BRECON, on completion, joined the 6th Destroyer Flotilla of the Home Fleet on escort and patrol duties with the fleet and in the English Channel. On 28.6.43 she sailed for the Mediterranean as part of the escort for Convoy KMF17 which became part of the forces for the Sicily landings (10.7.43). She then joined the 58th

Destroyer Division until 4.44. During this time she acted as an escort and provided fire support during the Salerno landings (9.9.43), having a minor collision with the destroyer LAFOREY on 29.9.43. In company with EXMOOR, BLANKNEY and BLENCATHRA she sank U450 on 10.3.44 off Anzio. From 4.44 until 5.45 BRECON served with the 18th Destroyer Flotilla, being present on 15.8.44 as an escort during the South of France landings. On 19.9.44 she participated in the destruction of U407 south of Melos, and during 10.44 was part of the re-occupation force for the Aegean Islands. However, in 1.45 she was temporarily attached to the 21st Flotilla at Sheerness for escort duties, but was soon back in the Mediterranean refitting and undergoing trials at Malta until 5.45 when she returned to the UK.

After a brief stay in the UK, she sailed on 10.6.45 to join the East Indies Fleet where she was allocated to the newly formed 29th Destroyer Flotilla at Colombo on 26.8.45. BRECON was subsequently present at the re-occupation of Singapore. With the other vessels of the 29th Flotilla she sailed for the UK on 3.11.45 and arrived at Portsmouth 4.12.45. She reduced to Category 'B' Reserve at Portsmouth until 11.9.48 when she started a refit at Harland & Wolff's yard at Southampton. On completion of this refit on 29.4.49 she was reclassified as Category 'A' Reserve at Portsmouth, until placed on the Sales List on 22.1.56. After this time she was used as a fender ship. Five years later, on 14.8.61, she was approved for scrapping and subsequently handed over to BISCo. She arrived at the Faslane yard of Shipbreaking Industries on 17.9.62 for demolition.

BRISSENDEN seen at Malta during her Mediterranean service with the 3rd Destroyer Flotilla between 1945 and 1947   *(Brownell Collection)*

BRISSENDEN (L79)

After working-up, BRISSENDEN joined the Home Fleet as an escort for several months before joining the Mediterranean Fleet for Operation 'Husky', with the 58th Destroyer Division. However, on 13.7.43, she was in collision with BLANKNEY and suffered a deep V-shaped cut on the port bow, centred on frame 15, with damage extending to frames 9 to 18. She returned to the UK and repairs were undertaken at Liverpool between 21.8.43 and 2.10.43. She then joined the 15th Destroyer Flotilla at Plymouth, after briefly covering the final legs of Convoys RA54A and RA54B from Russia until 12.44.

Whilst with the 15th, BRISSENDEN with TANATSIDE, TALYBONT and WENSLEYDALE engaged the German torpedo boat T29 and minesweepers M156 and M206 off the Brittany coast on 5.2.44. M156 was damaged and was finally destroyed by air attack. On the night of 15-16.3.44, BRISSENDEN and MELBREAK, whilst escorting a convoy off Land's End, damaged the German motor torpedo boat S143.

On 'D' Day BRISSENDEN escorted one of the follow-up convoys of Force B. After further escort duties, she refitted at Pembroke Dock between 5.12.44 and 1.2.45 when she joined the 21st Destroyer Flotilla at Sheerness for the final months of the European War.

BRISSENDEN then returned to the Mediterranean and acted as a reserve for the East Indies Station, being under repair at Alexandria between 1.10.45 and 1.46. She again refitted at Malta between 15.4. and 29.6.46, on completion of which she joined the 3rd Destroyer Flotilla undertaking patrol duties off Palestine until 12.47. She reduced to Category 'A2' Reserve at Portsmouth on 19.6.48, remaining there until 1953, when she transferred to Lisahally in Northern Ireland in Category II Reserve. There was talk of selling her to Kuwait in 1958 and converting her to a Royal Yacht. This came to nothing and she was placed on the Sales List on 19.6.62. On 18.2.65, she was sold for £29,000 to Arnott Young & Co Ltd of Glasgow and arrived under tow at Dalmuir on 3.3.65 for demolition.

BROCKLESBY on 30.10.42 whilst serving with the 15th Destroyer Flotilla at Plymouth and shows a typical Type 1 layout
(N.H.B.)

BROCKLESBY (L42)

BROCKLESBY was to have the longest service life of any of the Hunts in the Royal Navy, not finally paying off until 1963 after over ten years service as an experimental frigate.

Her service began in 7.41 when she joined the 15th Destroyer Flotilla at Portsmouth where she was to serve until 2.43 when she joined the Mediterranean Fleet's 57th Destroyer Division as a convoy escort until 3.45. BROCKLESBY was then ordered back to Home Waters with five sisters to counter the inshore U-boat campaign, joining the 16th Destroyer Flotilla at Harwich until the end of hostilities.

She saw much active service, destroying two German aircraft whilst protecting a convoy off Trevose Head on 20.3.42 and eight days later was one of the escorts (with CLEVELAND, ATHERSTONE and TYNEDALE) for the survivors from the St. Nazaire Raid (MTBs 314 and MLs 270, 446) suffering heavy air attacks in the process. Subsequently, on 19.8.42 BROCKLESBY with SLAZAK escorted Group 4 of the Dieppe Raiding Force and suffered repeated hits from shore fire while undertaking supporting fire for Green Beach (Pourville). During the action she rescued 23 survivors of the German trawler UJ1404, that had been sunk. BROCKLESBY was under repair for nearly two months following the action off Dieppe. She was next in action again on the night of 13-14.10.42 when she was one of the destroyers attacking the raider KOMET. She was later in action against German convoys on 1.11.42 and 11.12.42 and in the latter engagement she was put out of action for five days by shells falling short.

After joining the Mediterranean Fleet, BROCKLEBY saw action during the invasion of Sicily, when she conveyed Admiral Sir Bertram Ramsay, General Eisenhower and General Montgomery on 12.7.43, and at Salerno on 9.9.43. On 4.8.43 she escorted the monitor ROBERTS which was bombarding the undercliff road and railway at Taormina. During 1944 she engaged the enemy on three occasions. The first was on the night of 22-23.8.44 when she engaged enemy E-boats attacking Ancona. The second was when with WHEATLAND she bombarded the harbour of Bar, 60 miles southeast of Dubrovnik on the night of 13-14.11.44 and finally she was one of the four destroyers that bombarded the enemy explosive motorboat base on the island of Lussinpiccolo on 3.12.44.

BROCKLESBY operated with the 16th Destroyer Flotilla for the final two months of the war. After showing the flag with SOUTHDOWN at Wilhelmshaven following the surrender in May 1945, she was non-operational at Portsmouth awaiting conversion to an air target training ship. Following this conversion, she operated at Rosyth until she reduced to Category 'B' Reserve at Portsmouth on 1.5.46. BROCKLESBY was to remain in reserve at Portsmouth until 1951 (Category 'C' Reserve after 1948). She was then refitted at Devonport during 1951/52 as an experimental ship joining the 2nd Training Squadron. BROCKLESBY served as a trials vessel for variable depth sonar until 1960. Whilst on trials with the prototype Type 192 VDS, she almost capsized whilst towing this weighty apparatus. Subsequently, she served as a training vessel/experimental ship and did not pay off until 22.6.63. On 21.10.68, she was sold to Shipbreaking Industries Ltd and arrived at Faslane on 28.10.68, the last of the Hunts in Royal Navy service.

BROCKLESBY, whilst laid-up and disarmed as an Air Target Training Ship, on 27.2.52 and prior to her conversion to a trials vessel   *(N.H.B.)*

CALPE (L71)

On commissioning on 11.12.41, CALPE joined the First Destroyer Flotilla, where she was to serve for almost a year. The highlight of this period was her presence at the Dieppe Raid on 19.8.42 when she embarked the naval and military force commanders and sustained slight damage due to air attack.

CALPE was a reinforcement for the 'Torch' operation and was to serve in the Mediterranean until 10.44, with the 59th Destroyer Division (to 8.43), 48th Escort Group (8.43-9.43), 50th Escort Group (9.43-11.43), Mediterranean Hunts (11.43-12.43) and finally the 18th Destroyer Flotilla. During this period, CALPE was an escort at the Sicily Landings and on 12.12.43 with USS NIBLACK, WAINWRIGHT, BENSON and her sister HOLCOMBE sank U593 off the Algerian coast. U593 had previously sunk HMS TYNEDALE (qv) and during the action sank the HOLCOMBE. 1944 was to see CALPE engaged in the South of France Landings and she was one of the ships carrying the occupying forces to the Aegean islands during 10.44.

A typical Type 2 vessel, CALPE is seen here still carrying her searchlight. Post-war she became the Danish ROLF KRAKE   *(Brownell Collection)*

After a brief return to the UK, CALPE started a refit at Ferryville, Tunisia on 3.1.45 which took three months. After further repairs at Malta she returned home to Chatham on 11.5.45, although at this time she was nominally part of the 18th Destroyer Flotilla. After giving leave she made passage to the Far East and was on station at Trincomalee on VJ Day.

She then quickly returned to the UK and paid off into Category 'B' Reserve at Sheerness on 17.1.46. After refitting at Sheerness she re-joined reserve (Category B2) at Chatham during 1.47 and was later transferred to Portsmouth and then Harwich where she reduced to Category 'C' Reserve in 1950. CALPE was transferred to Sheerness in 1952 in preparation for her transfer on loan to Denmark as ROLF KRAKE. The loan period which commenced on 28.2.52 was extended first on 2.12.57 and then on 14.8.61 until 3.66. ROLF KRAKE was sold on 26.10.66 to Otto Danielsen for demolition in Denmark.

CATTERICK leaving Barrow Docks on completion during 6.42 *(N.H.B.)*

CATTERICK (L81)

CATTERICK was one of the most travelled of the 'Hunts', seeing service in West Africa, South and East Africa, as well as the Mediterranean.

When working up at Scapa in 6.42, she formed part of a diversionary convoy for the disastrous PQ17 operation. Thereafter, on completion of her work-up, she sailed as one of the escorts for Convoy WS21 to Freetown, rounding the Cape to join the Eastern Fleet's 2nd Destroyer Flotilla on 17.9.42. She had hardly settled in when, a month later, she was detached for convoy escort duties in South African waters until 4.43. During this time, she rescued 157 survivors from the SS LLANDAFF CASTLE, which had been torpedoed by U177 on 30.11.42.

Another view of CATTERICK leaving Barrow   (N.H.B.)

After a brief refit at Durban, CATTERICK left there on 16.4.43 as escort for the battleship WARSPITE. CATTERICK was to spend the next four months escorting convoys between Capetown and Freetown. She finally left Freetown on 24.8.43 for Gibraltar with Convoy CF13, arriving at Malta in time to participate in Operation 'Avalanche', the landings at Salerno on 8.9.43.

CATTERICK then operated in the Mediterranean with the 50th Escort Division (at Algiers between 9.43-11.43), with the Mediterranean Hunts (11.43-12.43), the 18th Destroyer Flotilla (Malta 12.43-12.44) and finally the 22nd Destroyer Flotilla at Alexandria between 12.44 and 5.45. She was largely employed on convoy escort duties, but acted as an escort for the South of France Landings and during the re-occupation of the Aegean islands during 10.44.

CATTERICK briefly returned home to give leave of her crew and in 7.45 left for Durban to refit for duty in the Far East. CATTERICK refitted at Durban until 31.1.46 when she sailed for Malta, arriving on 1.3.46. At Malta, CATTERICK was transferred on loan to the Royal Hellenic Navy as the ADMIRAL HASTINGS. She was to serve with the Greeks until 12.12.59 when she was discarded and subsequently scrapped at Piraeus during 7.63.

CATTISTOCK (L35)

While working up during 8.40, CATTISTOCK joined the 3rd Destroyer Flotilla at Scapa Flow, undertaking convoy escort and local patrols. On 3.9.40, a month after commissioning, she joined the 21st Destroyer Flotilla at Sheerness, where she was to be based for the whole of the war on coastal convoy escort and anti-E boat duties. She was engaged in many minor actions, which included the escorting of the monitor EREBUS when she bombarded invasion barges at Dunkirk on 12.10.40; she received splinter damage from aircraft bombs on 10.11.40.

CATTISTOCK, a Type 1, in 7.41. Note the absence of any electronic equipment and the simple pole type foremast   (N.H.B.)

During 1941, CATTISTOCK was near-missed and slightly damaged by bombs on 11.3.41 and six days later participated in an indecisive action with E-boats off the Humber. On 26.7.41 she joined QUORN and MENDIP in a bombardment of Dieppe. CATTISTOCK was again in action with E-boats off East Anglia on 12.4.42 but apart from supporting two offensive minelaying operations off the coast of Brittany in 5.43, her next two years were spent on convoy escort duties.

'D' Day saw CATTISTOCK attached to Force 'G' and providing gunfire support for 'Gold' Beach. Following these duties she was used on cross-channel escort work and on the night of 7-8.7.44, with LA COMBATTANTE and the frigate THORNBOROUGH, she was in action off Normandy with the German E-boats S167, S168, S174, S175, S176, S177, S180, S181 and S182. After a maintenance period between 31.7 and 24.8.44 at Portsmouth when her superheaters were retubed, CATTISTOCK returned to her duties. Five days later on the 29-30.8.44, she attempted with the frigate RETALICK to intercept a convoy of German landing craft and minesweepers fleeing from Le Havre and Fécamp.

CATTISTOCK suffered 26 hits, resulting in her forward 4" gun and radars being put out of action. Her Captain (Lt R. G. D. Keddie DSC) was killed and she required repairs lasting seven weeks at Chatham but returned to service in time to attack and probably sink a midget submarine off Zeebrugge on 2.2.45. After a period at Harwich, CATTISTOCK transferred to the Portsmouth Command in 8.45, visiting the Channel Islands in 9.45 and making three round trips to Gibraltar before finally returning to base on 6.12.45.

She reduced to Category 'B' Reserve at Devonport on 26.3.46 and was to remain there until 1950. In 1.50 a proposed loan to Norway was not pursued and CATTISTOCK remained in Reserve, latterly at Cardiff until approved for scrapping on 11.10.56. A week later she commenced de-equipping before being handed to BISCo for demolition. She arrived at John Cashmore's yard at Newport on 2.7.57 for breaking up.

A fine war-time view of CHIDDINGFOLD. She is not fitted with a Type 271 surface warning radar, but the Type 285 gunnery radar is present on the range finder   (Brownell Collection)

CHIDDINGFOLD (L31)

During her work-up, CHIDDINGFOLD was used as an escort for Operation 'Archery' — the raid on Vaagsfjord, Lofoten between 22.12.41 and 1.1.42. During the raid she bombarded enemy positions to cover the landings; with the destroyer OFFA she sank the German patrol vessel DONNER (V5102) and the 5,870 ton freighter ANHALT. On her return to Scapa, CHIDDINGFOLD was allocated to the Orkney and Shetland Command and her patrol and escort duties took her to Iceland, the Clyde and Rosyth. After refitting at Middlesbrough between 18.6.43 and 21.8.43, she was despatched to the Mediterranean where she served with the 59th Destroyer Division until 6.44 and later with the 22nd Flotilla.

CHIDDINGFOLD escorted convoys to ports in Italy, provided bombardment support for the Army and undertook operations to intercept German shipping off the coast of Dalmatia. After participating in the bombardment of Genoa on 1.3.45, she was ordered two days later to return to the UK to join the 16th Destroyer Flotilla at Harwich, to reinforce the anti-submarine protection of convoys to the Scheldt until the end of the war.

Following modifications at London between 29.5.45 and 2.7.45 for East Indies service, CHIDDINGFOLD worked up in the Mediterranean. She was present with the 18th Destroyer Flotilla at the occupation of Singapore during 9.45. CHIDDINGFOLD returned to Portsmouth on 16.11.45 and reduced to Category 'B' Reserve there on 25.3.46. In 1950 she was transferred to Harwich, still in reserve, until 17.6.52 when approval was given for her to be loaned to India for three years.

CHIDDINGFOLD was towed to Liverpool during 7.52 for refitting by Messrs Crichton, and this was completed on 9.6.53. She had meanwhile been renamed GANGA on 27.11.52 but was not formally transferred to India until 18.6.53. GANGA's loan period was extended on 28.5.56 and she was bought outright by the Indian Government on 8.4.58, serving with the Indian Navy as a training vessel until 1975, when she and her sister GOMATI (ex LAMERTON) were paid off and later scrapped.

CLEVELAND working-up at Scapa in 10.40 *(N.M.M.)*

CLEVELAND (L46)

After her work-up, CLEVELAND had a brief sojourn with the 23rd Destroyer Flotilla of the Home Fleet, the highlight of which was the rescue of 29 survivors from SS CONAKRIAN which had been torpedoed by German aircraft off Girdleness on 20.10.40. She then joined the First Destroyer Flotilla at Portsmouth for six months until 5.41. Her primary duty during this time was to escort convoys through the Straits of Dover, but she did take the offensive in 3.41 when she escorted destroyer-minelayers on a sortie off the French coast.

On her transfer to the 15th Destroyer Flotilla, where CLEVELAND was to spend nearly two years, her primary duty was to escort coastal convoys between Falmouth and Milford Haven. During this period, CLEVELAND rescued ten men from the armed yacht VIVA II which had been sunk off Trevose Head on 8.5.41. On 12.2.42 she was patrolling off Beachy Head during the Channel Dash but made no contact. Later she was one of the destroyers supporting the raid on St. Nazaire on 23.3.42. She spent most of that day under air attack while searching for ML's which had taken part in the raid and had not returned with the main force. On 16.5.42 CLEVELAND with BROCKLESBY shot down a German Me109 off Rame Head, Plymouth. CLEVELAND, as part of the escort for Convoy PW219 of nine ships, was attacked by E-boats off the Eddystone Lighthouse on the night of 17-18.9.42. She was missed by a torpedo, but suffered three casualties from gunfire. The convoy escaped unscathed. She left her station during 11.42 and escorted Convoy KMS2 to Gibraltar, returning home as escort for Convoy MKF1.

Following a collision on 19.2.43, CLEVELAND refitted at Dundee until 28.4.43 leaving the UK a month later as one of the escorts for Convoy KMF15/WS30 on her way to join the 57th Destroyer Division of the Mediterranean Fleet where she was based at Algiers. She was to remain with the Mediterranean Fleet until 9.45, seeing service with the 57th Division until 9.43, the 48th Escort Group during 9-10.43, the Malta Hunts 10.43-2.44, 18th Destroyer Flotilla Malta (until 10.44) and finally the 5th Destroyer Flotilla at Alexandria until the war's end. Her primary duties were those of convoy escort but she was present at the Sicily and Salerno

Landings where she formed part of the escort for the battleship WARSPITE. Between 9-16.8.44 she was a convoy escort for the South of France Landings and on 3.10.44 with CALPE sank six large assault craft off the island of Piscopi on the north-west coast of Rhodes. On 17.10.44 CLEVELAND with the destroyer landed a naval landing party at Scarpanto and finally on 1.3.45 bombarded Genoa docks with CHIDDINGFOLD.

She left Gibraltar on 25.9.45 to pay off into Category 'B' Reserve at Portsmouth and was to remain in this state until 12.48 when she was relegated to Category 'C' Reserve. She was to spend her last years in Extended Reserve at Cardiff until approved for disposal on 11.10.56. In 6.57, she was allocated to BISCo, but, whilst being towed to the breakers at Llanelli, she went ashore at Rhossili on the Gower Peninsula on the 28th of

Two views of CLEVELAND taken in 11.42. Note the change of camouflage and the presence (above) and absence (below) of a mainmast. Presumably the main mast was removed to improve the arches of fire of the 2pdr pom pom   *(both N.H.B.)*

that month. She was scrapped in situ over the next two years by Metal Trading (Swansea) Ltd. Work was completed by 14.12.59. Total towage and breaking costs were £12,700. The total amount recovered from insurance underwriters was £15,600. The net proceeds from scrapping were £14,900.

CLEVELAND aground at Rhosilli Sands. Demolition has already commenced   (W.S.P.L.)

COTSWOLD (L54)

COTSWOLD served with the 16th Destroyer Flotilla at Harwich for the whole of the war, but was lucky to survive the war, being seriously damaged by a mine and also involved in one serious and two slight collisions. The first of these collisions occurred during 3.41, when she sank the trawler ST DONATS. She then spent a month undergoing repair, but soon returned to her patrol and escort duties. COTSWOLD's mining occurred at 0950 hours on 20.4.42 when she was off Orfordness, at position 52.06 N 01.51 E. The explosion occurred under the stabiliser compartment between frames 37 and 44. All compartments below the lower deck were flooded and partial flooding occurred to compartments above the lower deck between stations 37-56. The boiler room flooded within 3 ft of the upper deck; steam was lost two minutes after the explosion had occurred and all lighting failed. Four of her crew were presumed lost. The destroyer LEEDS took COTSWOLD in tow at 1225, but an hour later the tug KENIA and salvage vessel DAPPER were secured alongside and at 1418 hours the tug SUPERMAN replaced the LEEDS which had towed COTSWOLD 14½ miles. At 1700 hours she was beached at Shotley Spit. On 3.5.42 she was refloated and tied up alongside Parkeston Quay and towed the next day by DAPPER and KENIA for Chatham and repairs.

Damage repairs were not completed until 8.5.43, when she rejoined the 16th Destroyer Flotilla. This service lasted until 24.10.43, when she was badly damaged in collision with the destroyer MONTROSE. Both boiler rooms, the engine room and the gearing room were flooded. The Lewis gun platform, searchlight platform and superstructure were also badly damaged.

Again, repairs took over six months and COTSWOLD did not rejoin the 16th Destroyer Flotilla until 9.5.44, seeing service off Normandy on 6.6.44. Her service was once again disrupted by a collision with SS CHIGNECTO PARK on 8.9.44 which necessitated a month's repair at Immingham.

COTSWOLD on 30.10.41 after nearly a year's service and yet to be fitted with radar   *(N.H.B.)*

On the night of 14-15.1.45, COTSWOLD with the frigate CURZON fought off an attack by the German 6th MTB Flotilla on a convoy west of the Scheldt. This was her final action of the war. She was then refitted at Portsmouth between 8.11.45 and 20.3.46, and entered Category 'B' Reserve at Harwich on 29.6.46. Remaining at Harwich, she was relegated to Category 'C' Reserve in 12.48 and this lasted until 1953 when she transferred to Extended Reserve at Barrow. On 16.1.56 she was downgraded to hulk status at Harwich in company with MIDDLETON, HAMBLEDON and WHEATLAND. In 8.57, she was allocated to BISCo for scrapping and arrived at the Grays, Essex, yard of T. W. Ward on 11.9.57. Demolition was completed by 7.3.58.

COTSWOLD pictured at the end of her career, whilst in tow for the breakers. Note the cocooned equipment
(W.S.P.L. Osbon)

COTTESMORE in 11.45 whilst serving briefly with the Portsmouth Local Flotilla. She was laid-up in reserve in 2.46 *(W.S.S. Kennedy)*

COTTESMORE (L78)

COTTESMORE was to serve as a member of the 21st Destroyer Flotilla at Sheerness for the whole of her war career. During this time she escorted East Coast convoys, undertook offensive patrols and covered coastal forces and minelaying operations. On 12.2.42 in company with other Nore destroyers, COTTESMORE attempted to intercept the SCHARNHORST and GNEISENAU, but did not make contact because of poor visibility. On 28.7.42 however, COTTESMORE and CALPE sank the German armed trawlers VP202 and VP203 off Cap de la Hague. Both Hunts were attacked by enemy aircraft during their return and COTTESMORE sustained slight damage and three casualties.

Three months later on the night of 13-14.10.42, COTTESMORE led QUORN, GLAISDALE, ESKDALE (RNN) and ALBRIGHTON from Dartmouth to a position off Cap de la Hague. In the early hours of 14.10.42, the flotilla encountered the German raider KOMET and in the action that followed, the five Hunts severely damaged the four escorting torpedo boats, while MTB 236 torpedoed and sank the raider.

On D-Day, COTTESMORE escorted part of the 150th BYMS Flotilla and the 18th Minesweeping Flotilla to a point off 'GOLD' Beach. When the channels had been cleared, she acted as a gunfire support vessel. After the initial phase, she remained based at Portsmouth, escorting the reinforcement convoys and patrolling off the beaches to intercept E-boats and midget submarines until 8.44. In 11.44 COTTESMORE and GARTH escorted the monitors EREBUS and ROBERTS while they engaged coastal batteries on Walcheren Island. At the end of the war COTTESMORE escorted British minesweepers to Cuxhaven and then joined the Harwich Force until 8.45. She then joined the Portsmouth Flotilla until 28.2.46 when she reduced to Category 'B' Reserve at Devonport, reducing to Category 'C' Reserve there in 1.49.

On 31.1.50 she was offered to the Egyptian Government as she lay for £120,000 exclusive of naval and armament stores valued at £32,000 and £51,000 respectively. On 20.4.50 Egypt accepted the offer and announced that the ship was to be refitted by White's at Cowes. On 17.7.50 she was towed to Cowes and renamed IBRAHIM EL AWAL, but was renamed MOHAMED ALI six months later. After refitting she served as a training vessel at Port Said, being later renamed PORT SAID and was in 1986 the last Hunt in service.

COWDRAY (L52)

COWDRAY, despite being completed in mid 1942, was to see scarcely three months active service during the war. After working up, she joined the Londonderry Special Escort Division in 9.42 and undertook escort duties during the North African invasion. On 8.11.42 at 1715 hours, whilst engaged on A/S patrol off 'C' Beach east of Cape Natifou, Algeria, COWDRAY was subject to a co-ordinated torpedo and bomb attack by 12 aircraft. The torpedoes missed, but COWDRAY was hit by a 500 kg bomb which struck her on the starboard edge of the forecastle between frames 38 and 40, passed through the upper and lower decks and through the bottom of the vessel between frames 41 and 43 before exploding under No 1 boiler room between frames 58 to 60. The ship was extensively damaged with hull plating under the boiler room being blown upwards 12 ft and side plating seriously damaged. The forecastle deck was corrugated and the No 1 boiler room and auxiliary machinery were wrecked or seriously damaged. She was immobilised but was taken in tow by the minesweeper ALGERINE at 1840 hours, having lost five killed and 12 wounded. As the situation at Algiers was not known, all confidential papers were jettisoned and demolition charges were placed in the transmitting and radar compartments. At 1600 hours on 9.11.42, she was beached about 7 miles from Algiers and abandoned. A week later however, on 16.11.42, COWDRAY was towed clear, down by the bows, and entered Algiers, being berthed next to the AA ship PALOMARES.

COWDRAY on 16.7.47 whilst operating with the Nore Flotilla *(N.M.M)*

During the ensuing five months temporary repairs were undertaken, these included renewing plating and making the fuel tanks serviceable. On trials, subsequently, the ship had a hog amidships to a maximum of about 2″.

COWDRAY sailed from Algiers for home on 24.4.43, arriving at Chatham on 22.5.43 where repairs were in hand between 2.6.43 and 23.9.44. Whilst under repair it was proposed to transfer COWDRAY to the Royal Hellenic Navy as the ADMIRAL HASTINGS, but this proposal was dropped on 20.1.44 in favour of the ship continuing under RN control.

Following these lengthy repairs, COWDRAY worked up and joined the 21st Destroyer Flotilla in 11.44, but was on station barely two months before she hit a submerged wreck, whilst attacking a midget submarine on 10.1.45. This punctured her Asdic dome and damaged the propellers and shafts; the necessary repairs at Chatham were not completed until 12.4.45. Subsequently, COWDRAY was assigned to the East Indies Fleet at the end of the European war and after the necessary alterations and modifications, she set sail for Ceylon. However, she was still on passage when the war ended on 3.9.45. Returning to the UK, COWDRAY operated with the Nore Flotilla until paying off to Category 'A' Reserve at Chatham on 30.1.50. A few weeks previously she had rescued the few survivors from the submarine TRUCULENT, lost in collision in the Thames estuary.

COWDRAY was to remain in reserve, Category 'A' at Chatham between 1950-2, Category 'B' Reserve at Chatham 1952-3, Class I Reserve at Portsmouth between 1953-4, Class II Reserve at Hartlepool between 1954-5 and finally Supplementary Reserve at Hartlepool until she was towed to Gateshead and arrived at the yard of J. J. King and Sons on 3.9.59 for demolition.

CROOME (L62)

CROOME spent 7.41 working up at Scapa and she was then allocated to the 12th Escort Group of the Western Approaches Command on general escort and patrol duties until 2.42. During this period CROOME

CROOME, on 2.10.45, leaving Grand Harbour to return to the U.K. to reduce to reserve. Note the late war colour scheme *(Brownell Collection)*

54

participated in the sinking of two submarines, the first being the Italian BARACCA on 8.9.41, sunk by gunfire and ramming north-east of the Azores at position 40.15 N 20.55 W. CROOME was under repair between 12.9 and 4.10.41 as a consequence of the ramming. The second submarine destroyed was U127, which was attacked and sunk off Cape St Vincent on 14.12.41 by CROOME and the destroyers GURKHA, FOXHOUND and HMAS NESTOR.

Between February and April 1942, CROOME was attached to Force 'H' at Gibraltar and served as an escort when Force 'H' undertook three flying-off operations with aircraft for Malta. These operations occurred between 27-28.2.42 (aborted), 6.3-8.3.42 and 20.3-30.3.42.

CROOME then spent the next two months escorting convoys from Freetown but transferred to the Mediterranean Fleet in 6.42, serving with the 5th Destroyer Flotilla until 3.43 and then the 22nd Destroyer Flotilla until 9.44. During this period CROOME participated in the 'Vigorous' Malta convoy operation of 6.42, took part in the sinking of her third submarine (U372) off Haifa with ZULU, SIKH and TETCOTT on 4.8.42 and participated in the bombardment of Daba on 29.8.42. She also took part in the disastrous combined operations attack on Tobruk on the night of 13-14.9.42, when the cruiser COVENTRY and destroyers SIKH and ZULU were lost.

The latter months of 1942 were spent on convoying stores to Malta and convoy escort duties were to be her primary role for the rest of her service in the Mediterranean. She did, however, participate in the Salerno Landings of 9.43; the Aegean campaign of 10.43 by landing troops at Leros and the Anzio Landings of 1.44.

CROOME returned to home waters in late 1944, joining the 21st Destroyer Flotilla at Sheerness for three months, until 3.45. She then provided part of the escort for the light fleet carriers VENERABLE, VENGEANCE and COLOSSUS from the UK to the Mediterranean. CROOME was retained in the Mediterranean until 10.45, when she returned to Plymouth and reduced to Category 'B' Reserve.

She was to remain in reserve until her disposal (Category 'B1' at Plymouth in 1945/7 and later Categories 'B2' and 'C' until 1954, when she transferred to Cardiff and Class III Reserve for 1954/5 and finally Extended Reserve). CROOME was handed over to BISCo and arrived on 13.8.57 at T. W. Ward's Briton Ferry yard for breaking up.

DERWENT, a typical Type 3 on commissioning. She survived 11 months before being written-off by aerial torpedo at Tripoli on 19.3.43
(Brownell Collection)

DERWENT (L83)
The highlight of DERWENT's active career was as part of the escort of the 'Pedestal' Convoy to Malta, which entered the Mediterranean on 10.8.42. However, DERWENT with her sisters BICESTER and WILTON were detailed to Gibraltar as escort for the torpedoed cruiser NIGERIA.

Although nominally part of the 5th Destroyer Flotilla based at Alexandria from 29.6.42 until early 1943, DERWENT spent the next four months after 9.42 on the South African station, escorting convoys and major warships such as the battleship REVENGE between Durban and Kilindini. In 2.43, she was an escort for the convoy carrying the Ninth Australian Division through the Red Sea.

On 19.3.43 (as a new member of the 22nd Destroyer Flotilla), DERWENT was at anchor in Tripoli Harbour, when the port was attacked by 12 Ju88's and two merchant ships, OCEAN VOYAGER and VARVARA were set on fire. DERWENT, whilst weighing anchor to avoid these ships, was hit by a circling torpedo which blew a hole 28' × 16' in the port side at frame 69. Six members of the crew were killed. The boiler rooms were flooded and the ship suffered slow flooding in the engine room, low-power room and wardroom. Both boiler rooms were wrecked and the ship was completely immobilised as all steam and electrical power was lost. The ship's bilge and flat keels were also badly damaged.

After temporary repairs had been undertaken, DERWENT was towed home by the tug ALLEGIANCE as part of Convoy MKS18. Permanent repairs were started at Devonport on 11.8.43. Work progressed slowly until 1.45 when it was stopped. DERWENT reduced to Category 'C' Reserve on 20.7.45 and her machinery was removed between 7-9.46 for use at the Fleet Engineering College at Manadon. The damaged hulk of DERWENT was handed over to BISCo on 8.11.46 and demolition commenced on 21.2.47 at the Penryn yard of T. W. Ward.

DULVERTON appears on this picture to be picking up survivors, possibly from SOUTHWOLD. DULVERTON was to be one of the first vessels to be lost by glider bomb attack in the Aegean on 12.11.43

(Brownell Collection)

DULVERTON (L63)

After working up at Scapa during 10.41, DULVERTON sailed as an additional escort for a troop convoy to the Cape and arrived on station with the 5th Destroyer Flotilla at Suez on 4.1.42. She was to serve with this flotilla until her loss 22 months later. During this period, in addition to undertaking general fleet and escort duties, she participated in the actions in Sirte Gulf. With her sisters EXMOOR, CROOME, ERIDGE, AIREDALE, BEAUFORT, HURWORTH, TETCOTT and ALDENHAM, she provided part of the escort for the 'Vigorous' Convoy from Alexandria to Malta. The convoy was forced to return because of heavy air attack. DULVERTON also bombarded Mersa Matruh on 12.7.42; and was part of the escort for the disastrous Commando Raid on Tobruk on the night of 13-14.9.42. She participated in the destruction of U559 on 30.10.42 and between 16-20.11.42 was part of the escort of the first convoy to arrive at Malta from Alexandria since March 1942.

In 1943, she was a regular escort for Malta Convoys until May, when she became part of the blockading force off Cape Bon. In 10.7.43 she was engaged in protecting the landings on Sicily and two months later undertook similar duties for the Salerno landings.

Between 20.10-4.11.43, she made three round trips to Leros with personnel and stores. On 12.11.43, after Leros had been invaded, DULVERTON returned with ECHO and BELVOIR to support the garrison at Leros. There, on the night of 13.11.43, whilst five miles from Leros, the three ships were attacked by DO217's of squadron 5 KG 100 and DULVERTON was hit by a Hs293 glider bomb. The entire bow structure forward of the bridge was torn away and the ship settled by the head. Six officers and 103 ratings were taken off and she was scuttled by BELVOIR two hours after the attack. Captain (D) of the Fifth Flotilla, two other officers and 75 ratings were lost with DULVERTON.

EASTON in 3.46 whilst serving with the 3rd Escort Flotilla at Portsmouth   *(Brownell Collection)*

EASTON (L09)

After completing her work-up at Scapa during 1.43, EASTON sailed for service with the 22nd Destroyer Flotilla at Alexandria. She was used on general patrol and escort duties until 8.43 being involved in the sinking of no less than four submarines during this period, three of them in a matter of 20 days during 2-3.43. On 17.2.43 with WHEATLAND, she sank the Italian submarine ASTERIA off Bougie, and six days later sank U443 off Algiers with BICESTER, LAMERTON and WHEATLAND. Subsequently U83 was damaged by EASTON and finished off by aircraft south of Cartagana on 9.3.43.

While on escort duties covering the build-up after the Sicily Landings, accompanied by RHN PINDOS, EASTON sighted U458 south of Pantellaria on 22.8.43. EASTON rammed U458 at 20 knots and succeeded in not only sinking the U-boat but considerably damaging herself as well. She was never quite the same vessel after this and it was to lead to her premature scrapping. In the collision, EASTON's bow from the keel to 3 feet below the upper deck and for 28' aft to frame 16 was torn away or buckled. Both propeller shafts and A brackets were also damaged.

After temporary repair at Malta, permanent repairs were not completed at Gibraltar until 18.9.44. EASTON then joined the 59th Destroyer Division, shelling Greek Communist positions near Piraeus between 5-9.12.44. She was then recalled home to join the 21st Destroyer Flotilla at Sheerness in 3.45 and after refitting at Southampton between 5-8.45, she entered Category 'B' Reserve on 29.10.45. EASTON re-entered service with the 3rd Escort Flotilla at Portsmouth during 1946/7, but spent considerable periods under repair, finally being relegated to Category 'B' Reserve at Harwich on 3.11.47. EASTON transferred to Sheerness for a refit, which commenced on 8.8.49. However, work stopped on 2.9.49 as EASTON's condition was so poor and on 4.11.49 she was allocated for service as a training hulk at Rosyth. She was stripped of equipment at Sheerness between 7.11 and 19.12.49 before transfer to Rosyth where she served as a hulk until 4.12.52 when she was allocated to Metal Industries Ltd and scrapped at their yard at Rosyth in 1.53.

A war view of EGGESFORD and showing her with a complete radar fit   *(Brownell Collection)*

This excellent late-war view (1944/45) of EGGESFORD shows in detail the Type 3 configuration

(N.M.M.)

EGGESFORD (L15)

EGGESFORD spent the first 20 months of her service in the Mediterranean, with the 60th Destroyer Division at Malta (3.43-7.44) and after a refit, from 8.44 to 11.44 with the 5th Destroyer Flotilla. During this time she was engaged at the invasions of Sicily, Italy and the south of France. EGGESFORD, although nominally part of the 18th Destroyer Flotilla, spent the last six months of the European War at the Nore with the 21st Destroyer Flotilla, not finally joining the 18th at Trincomalee until after VJ Day.

EGGESFORD returned home, but did not finally reduce to Category 'B1' Reserve at Portsmouth until 25.11.46 after a year's service with a training flotilla at Rosyth. EGGESFORD was destined to spend the next ten years in Reserve (Category 'B1' Reserve at Portsmouth until 5.1.49 and then Category 'C' at the same port until 4.11.52 when she was laid up at Penarth).

On 3.5.56 it was announced that EGGESFORD together with OAKLEY, ALBRIGHTON and the Black Swans ACTAEON, FLAMINGO, HART and MERMAID were earmarked for transfer to the new Federal German Navy. However, she was not formally sold to the West Germans until 11.11.57, when she was renamed BROMMY. After refit at Pembroke Dock, BROMMY commissioned on 14.5.59 as a training ship for underwater weapons and was not finally broken up in Germany until 1979.

EGLINTON (L87)

After work-up, EGLINTON joined the 16th Destroyer Flotilla at Harwich for the whole of the war and saw no overseas service at all. She was one of the unsung escorts that kept the perilous East Coast convoys protected, but hardly ever became news-worthy. On 28.7.43 she was in collision with SHELDRAKE and received bow damage that necessitated repairs at Chatham until 12.9.43. She was in two actions with E-boats, the first of these being on the night of 24-25.10.43, when EGLINTON, with PYTCHLEY, WORCESTER, CAMPBELL, MACKAY, six MGB's and two ML's escorting convoy FN1160, were attacked by 32 'S' boats of the 2nd, 4th, 6th and 8th Flotilla's off Cromer. The S boats were driven off with the loss of the trawler WILLIAM STEPHEN. Exactly four months later, EGLINTON and VIVIEN drove off S boats of the 2nd and 8th Flotillas which were attacking convoy FS1371.

EGLINTON — a war view showing the ship in some detail   *(I.W.M.)*

Besides duties with the Support Force off 'Sword' Beach during the 'D' Day Landings, EGLINTON continued her escort duties until the end of the war. EGLINTON saw no further active service with the Royal Navy, being in Category 'B2' Reserve at Harwich until 1950, followed by a further period of Extended Reserve at Portsmouth and later Hartlepool. She refitted at Hull during 1952 and was re-activated briefly in 6.55 as part of the 'Sleeping Beauty' exercise. On 28.5.56 EGLINTON arrived at Blyth for demolition by Hughes Bolckow.

ERIDGE (L68)

ERIDGE was the first of the Type 2's to complete in 2.41 and after initial work-up and service with the Irish Sea Escort Force, she arrived at Gibraltar on 21.6.41 to join the 13th Destroyer Flotilla. She was then attached to Force 'X' for Operation 'Substance' — a supply convoy from Gibraltar to Malta. However, on 23.7.41, ERIDGE was detached to tow the damaged destroyer FIREDRAKE to Gibraltar, arriving there on 27.7.41. On 30.7.41 she was part of the escort for the battleship NELSON taking supplies and personnel for Malta.

After circumnavigating Africa in company with AVON VALE, ERIDGE arrived at Suez on 29.9.41 and joined the Second Destroyer Flotilla until 11.41, when she was attached to the 5th Destroyer Flotilla at Alexandria where she remained for the rest of her service. In the next nine months, ERIDGE was involved in a number of major actions — between 12.2-6.2.42 as an escort of convoy MW9A from Alexandria to Malta; between 20.3-23.3.42 as an escort for the convoy MF1 and being present at the Battle of Sirte where she attempted unsuccessfully to tow her sister HEYTHROP after the latter had been torpedoed by U652 on 20.3.42. She also rescued over 100 survivors from the transport CLAN CAMPBELL on 23.3.42. Then on 28.5.42, whilst on escort duty with convoy AT47 and in company with HERO and HURWORTH, she sank U568 about 100 miles NE of Tobruk and picked up 42 survivors. In 6.42 ERIDGE took part in Operation 'Vigorous' and on 12.7.42 whilst covering a bombardment of Mersa Matruh, she assisted in sinking the German ammunition ship STURLA (1,397 tons).

However, on 29.8.42 whilst bombarding Daba, ERIDGE was hit by a torpedo fired by a small torpedo boat. A 20 ft hole was blown from keel level to within 3 ft of the upper deck. The ship was immobilised by the complete loss of electrical power and by the flooding of the engine room and gearing room. She was towed to Alexandria by ALDENHAM but was decommissioned in 9.42 and declared a constructive total loss because of the following damage:

1. The port side plating distorted between frames 90-112.
2. The keel severely distorted and forced up between frames 88 and 108.
3. Lower deck buckled between frames 105-114.
4. The starboard main turbines, condenser, gearing and intermediate shaft were damaged beyond repair.

ERIDGE was used as an accommodation ship at Alexandria until 10.46 when she was sold to Gasvialidis & Heliopolis and scrapped at Alexandria.

ESKDALE (Nor) photographed in the Mersey following her completion in 7.42   *(N.H.B.)*

Norwegian ESKDALE (L36)

On 8.6.42 it was agreed that the Royal Norwegian Navy would take over ESKDALE in place of the destroyer NEWPORT, which would be placed in Care and Maintenance by the Royal Navy. ESKDALE commissioned with her Norwegian crew on 20.7.42 and after working up at Scapa Flow, she joined the First Destroyer Flotilla at Portsmouth during 9.42. She was to serve in this Flotilla on escort and patrol duties until her loss.

ESKDALE was present at the 'KOMET' action in the Channel on 13-14.10.42 and was damaged in the wheelhouse and director in an action off Dieppe on 12.12.42, when she had to be steered from the emergency conning position aft. After this action, she was under repair at Portsmouth until 16.1.43. However, her end came when she was hit by two of the torpedoes fired by the German MTB's S90, S112 and S65 of the German 5th Flotilla when she was escorting Convoy PW232 of six ships off the Lizard on 14.4.43.

EXMOOR (I) (L61)

EXMOOR's work-up at Scapa was interrupted by the need to undertake urgent escort duties, and between 6.11.-13.11.40 with PYTCHLEY, she escorted the SS ADDA to the Faroes and during December with COTSWOLD, she escorted the AMC's CHITRAL and SALOPIAN to join the Northern Patrol. Finally she escorted the battleship QUEEN ELIZABETH from Portsmouth to Rosyth to complete her reconstruction. EXMOOR then joined the 16th Destroyer Flotilla at Harwich for what were to be the final two months of her service. On 25.2.41 she left Harwich as an additional escort for convoy FN417 (from the Thames to Firth of Forth). At 2115 hours on the 25th, EXMOOR was sunk by an explosion off Lowestoft in position 52.29 N 01.50 E (German sources suggest that she was torpedoed by the motor torpedo boat S30, however British sources suggest that the explosion was caused by a mine). The explosion split the hull, causing severe internal damage from the tiller-flat to the engine room. Oil fuel, which had been sprayed over the after-end by the explosion, ignited and the after-end was enveloped in flames and the fire spread rapidly forward. EXMOOR finally capsized to port, stood on end and sank in ten minutes. Her survivors were rescued by the patrol vessel SHEARWATER and the trawler COMMANDER EVANS and were subsequently landed at Yarmouth.

EXMOOR (II) (ex BURTON) (L08)

BURTON was renamed EXMOOR during 6.41 after the previous EXMOOR's loss. After her trials and work-up, EXMOOR was attached to Force 'H' at Gibraltar during 12.41 for three months. During this period, she participated in the sinking of U131 on 17.12.41. She then undertook fleet and convoy escort duties with the 37th Destroyer Division at Gibraltar until 6.42. The highlights of this period of her service was to act as an escort for aircraft carriers, flying-off aircraft to Malta, in 3.42, as well as participating as an escort for the 'Vigorous' Convoy operation to Malta in June.

EXMOOR (II) launched as BURTON, she was renamed in 6.41 to perpetuate the name of the first Hunt lost
(Brownell Collection)

EXMOOR then transferred to the eastern Mediterranean, where she served with the 5th and later the 22nd Destroyer Flotillas for the remainder of the war. She was employed on escort duties, but did see action on several occasions. On the night of 11-12.7.43, during the invasion of Sicily, EXMOOR with the destroyers KANARIS and ESKIMO, was beaten off by heavy gunfire while attempting to enter Augusta harbour. 9.43, saw EXMOOR engaged on convoy operations supporting the Salerno landings and during the autumn of that year she was engaged in the Aegean. On 10.3.44, EXMOOR with BLANKNEY, BLENCATHRA and BRECON sank U450 off Anzio.

After refitting in the summer of 1945, she was one of several Hunts held in reserve in the Mediterranean for possible service in the Far East. EXMOOR with HAYDON was held at Malta, whilst CROOME was at Ferryville, Tunisia and AVON VALE and STEVENSTONE were both held at Alexandria and BRISSENDEN at Piraeus.

EXMOOR returned to the UK and reduced to Category 'B' Reserve at Portsmouth on 10.11.45. She remained in reserve (Category 'B2' in 1947 and Category 'C' in 1949) until her sale to the Royal Danish Navy in 1952 as VALDEMAR SEJR. Whilst in Danish service she was refitted in 1953/4 with six 4" and three 40 mm guns with two depth charge throwers. She was stricken during 2.62, finally being sold on 26.10.66 to O. Danielsen for breaking up.

EXMOOR (II) disarmed prior to her transfer to the Royal Dutch Navy as VALDEMAR SEJR in 1952
(W.S.P.L. Kennedy)

FARNDALE pictured on 26.2.47 when part of the Nore Local Flotilla between 1946-50   *(N.H.B.)*

FARNDALE (L70)

After her work-up FARNDALE served with the 13th Destroyer Flotilla at Gibraltar on general escort duties but did participate as an escort on two Malta convoys — Operation 'Substance' in July and Operation 'Halberd' in September of 1941, as well as several aircraft ferrying missions. She was then ordered to join the 22nd Destroyer Flotilla at Alexandria, which she did on 17.10.41 after rounding the Cape. FARNDALE was engaged on escorting convoys to Tobruk until 2.42 and whilst engaged on these duties she sank the Italian submarine CARACCIOLO off Bardia on 11.12.41. However, on 9.2.42, when west of Mersa Matruh, FARNDALE was seriously damaged and immobilised by a 500 lb bomb which exploded beneath her and flooded her boiler rooms and the compartments between frames 37 and 56. The corvette GLOXINIA towed her into Mersa Matruh two days later. After temporary damage repairs at Alexandria to 8.3.42, FARNDALE sailed via the Cape to the UK for permanent repairs that were undertaken at London between 2.5.-8.8.42.

After escorting Convoy PQ18 to Iceland during 9.42, FARNDALE went south and was engaged in gunfire support duties at Oran in 11.42. These invasion duties were the start of a two year spell in the Mediterranean during which she participated in the invasions of Sicily, Italy and South of France and the ill-fated Aegean Campaign during October and November 1943. During this campaign she suffered damage from shore batteries.

FARNDALE then joined the 16th Destroyer Flotilla at Harwich in 11.44 and stayed until the end of the war being engaged on convoy duties between the Thames and the Scheldt. On the night of 14-15.1.45 she was in action against the German S boats S98, S92 and S48 off the Humber. After tropical modifications, FARNDALE sailed to join the 18th Flotilla at Trincomalee during July and participated in the Port Swettenham Landings of 9.45. After VJ Day, FARNDALE promptly returned to the UK and paid off into the Reserve during November; however she was quickly re-activated in 1946 to join the Nore Flotilla for the next five years. FARNDALE was then laid up in Category 'B' Reserve at Chatham until 12.54 when she was towed to the Tyne to be de-humidified. She was then laid-up at North Shields, with COWDRAY, between 4.56 and 8.57 when she joined the Supplementary Reserve at Hartlepool until 11.62. On the 29th of that month FARNDALE arrived at the Blyth yard of Hughes Bolckow for demolition.

FERNIE, in 2.43, shortly after joining the 21st Destroyer Flotilla at Sheerness, where she served until 5.45
(N.H.B.)

FERNIE (L11)

After working up, FERNIE was briefly attached to the 3rd Destroyer Flotilla of the Home Fleet and assisted in the evacuation of Le Havre and Cherbourg during 6.40 before joining the First Destroyer Flotilla at Portsmouth until 12.42. Beside the usual escort and patrol duties, FERNIE participated in the search for SCHARNHORST and GNEISENAU during the Channel Dash on 15.2.42. On the night of 13-14.3.42 she was damaged in action with the raider 'MICHEL' and the torpedo boats SEEADLER, ILTIS, JAGUAR, FALKE and KONDOR. She was also engaged in the Dieppe Raid (19.8.42) and the successful action on the night of 13-14.10.42 when the raider 'KOMET' was sunk. FERNIE spent the final years of the war on escort and patrol duties with the 21st Destroyer Flotilla at Sheerness, participating in the Normandy Landings. On 18.1.45 with LST 239 she rescued the crew of SS SAMVERN.

During 8.45 FERNIE was designated as an aircraft target ship at Rosyth being disarmed six months later. She remained on these duties until 1947 when she reduced to Category 'C' Reserve at Harwich. FERNIE then reduced to Class III Reserve at Barrow during 1953 and two years later further reduced to Extended Reserve. She remained at Barrow until 11.56 and finally arrived on the seventh of that month at Port Glasgow for demolition, by Smith and Houston.

Seen here as a disarmed target in 4.46, FERNIE served in this role until 1947, when she entered reserve. She was to remain in reserve until broken up during 11.56
W.S.P.L. (Kennedy)

This fine action photograph of GARTH was taken in 8.40 during her service with the 21st Destroyer Flotilla

(Maritime Photo Library)

GARTH (L20)

GARTH spent the whole of the war on east coast escort duties, serving with the 21st Destroyer Flotilla for the majority of that period. Her only detachments were with Rosyth Command between May and August 1941 and the 16th Destroyer Flotilla between April and August 1942.

However, she twice escorted the monitor EREBUS whilst the latter was engaged on bombardment duties off Calais (30.9.40) and Dunkirk (15.10.40). A month later on 20.11.40, with the destroyer CAMPBELL, she sank the German motor torpedo boat S38 off Southwold. GARTH was to sink another MTB (S71) off Lowestoft on the night of the 17-18.2.43 by gunfire and ramming. In the meanwhile, GARTH was one of the eight Hunts used as an escort for the ill-fated raid at Dieppe, as part of Operation 'Jubilee', where she bombarded the east cliff of 'BLUE' Beach.

After a further period of escort duties, interrupted by supporting a force of motor launches minelaying off Sark in 5.43, GARTH towed the escort carrier SLINGER back to Sheerness on 5.2.44, after the latter had been mined on passage from Sheerness to the Clyde. A fortnight later, on the night of 22-23.2.44, GARTH with SOUTHDOWN and MTB's 609 and 610 drove off German S-Boats which were attacking a convoy off Smith's Knoll. The German S94 and S128 were sunk by collision.

The final year of the war was spent on escort duties, but she formed part of Force 'L' on 'D' Day and with COTTESMORE gave supporting fire to the Walcheren landing on 1.10.44. October 1944, however, was also to see GARTH used to carry HM The King from Ostend to Dover on the 16th. GARTH was to see action twice more before the end of the war, first on 21.2.45 when she failed to stop German S-Boats torpedoing two vessels in the convoy she was escorting. However, on 14.4.45 she was more successful when she sank a midget submarine off Orfordness, taking two prisoners in the process.

During this period GARTH was damaged three times — the first time on 1.12.40 when she required a month's repair, after activating a mine in the Thames estuary. During 3.41, she received considerable damage when she grounded, being under repair at London until 5.41. Finally on 19.11.41, she was immobilised when hit in the boiler room by a 40 mm shell fired by another British destroyer. Again, repairs took a month.

On 25.5.45, GARTH conveyed the British Ambassador to the Netherlands to Rotterdam and remained as part of the Nore Local Flotilla until 12.45, when she paid off to act as accommodation ship at Sheerness for the next two years. She was in Category 'B' Reserve until 1949 and then Category 'C' Reserve until 1953 at Harwich, when she transferred to Supplementary Reserve at Barrow until disposal. GARTH was then broken up by T. W. Ward at Barrow; demolition beginning on 25.8.58. The net scrap realisation was £19,000. (Under the BISCo system, ships were not sold, but a net surplus was realised after breaking costs had been deducted).

GLAISDALE (L44)

GLAISDALE was transferred on 23.12.41 to the Royal Norwegian Navy whilst building and served with the Norwegians for all of her active career with the First Destroyer Flotilla at Portsmouth. Her only deployment overseas was to escort 'Torch' convoys to and from North Africa; finally returning home on 26.11.42. GLAISDALE was also engaged in the 'KOMET' action off Le Havre on the night of 13-14.10.42; the convoy action off the Lizard when her sister ESKDALE was lost (13-14.4.43) and finally on the night of 9-10.7.43 when, with WENSLEYDALE and MELBREAK, she engaged a German convoy near Ushant and sank the German minesweeper M135. However, GLAISDALE and MELBREAK were both damaged in this action by fire from the German torpedo boats T24 and T25.

GLAISDALE was another vessel taken over on completion in 6.42 by the Norwegians and served with them until damaged by a mine off Normandy two years later and reduced to reserve. Repaired, she was permanently transferred to Norway as NARVIK in 10.46   *(N.H.B. 6.42)*

After being on escort duty on 'D' Day, GLAISDALE was damaged 17 days later by an acoustic mine off the Normandy beaches. The explosion occurred about 45 ft off the starboard side abreast of the torpedo tubes. Seaworthiness was not affected, but the starboard engine was seriously damaged and after a survey she paid off into Category 'B' Reserve, being returned to the Royal Navy on 2.8.44. GLAISDALE remained in reserve at Hartlepool for exactly two years before her sale to Norway. After her armament had been replaced at Chatham, she was renamed NARVIK on 23.10.46, and finally arrived at Horten on 4.2.47 after working up in the UK. NARVIK remained on the effective list until 1.5.61 when she was stricken and subsequently broken up locally.

GOATHLAND (L27)

After her completion, which was delayed by bomb damage at Fairfield's during 3.41, GOATHLAND joined the 15th Destroyer Flotilla in 1.43 and saw all her active service as a destroyer with this unit. During this period, she was engaged in several actions, the first of which was an attempt to sink the raider 'TOGO' a few days after joining the Flotilla; and with ALBRIGHTON, GOATHLAND sank the Italian merchant ship BUTTERFLY off the Sept Iles and by her own 4" gunfire sank the trawler UJ1402 on the night of 27-28.4.43. In this action GOATHLAND was superficially hit. GOATHLAND engaged motor torpedo boats off Portland on 29.5.43 and again on 3.9.43 with LIMBOURNE. On 23.9.43 she commenced her conversion to an Assault Group HQ Ship at Liverpool. This entailed the following modifications:

1. An extra two-pounder bow chaser added for E-boat defence.
2. Her single Oerlikons were replaced by three twin mountings.
3. Additional accommodation and communications equipment was provided for the extra 107 crew after her conversion (284 total).

After completion of this conversion during 1.44, GOATHLAND worked up in the Moray Firth with the landing ships and army units of Force 'S'.

GOATHLAND on completion in 12.42. She served as a H.Q. ship off Normandy until declared a total loss after being mined on 24.7.44   *(N.H.B.)*

After the landings of 6.6.44 had been successfully completed, GOATHLAND became the HQ Ship for the Captain of Northbound Sailings during the day and patrolled the beaches at night. However, when on this duty, at 0423 hours on 24.7.44 she activated a ground mine. The explosion corrugated the hull plating for two-thirds of the ship's length but flooding was limited to the after magazine and fuel tank. Much shock damage occured to her turbines, gearing, boiler mountings and turbo-generators and both propeller shafts were bent and eventually seized.

At Portsmouth, after being towed in, her damage was described as widespread 'but not severe'. However, no long term repairs were undertaken and she seems to have fallen foul of the Royal Navy manning crisis. GOATHLAND was laid up at Inveraray between 10.44 and 2.45 and in the Gareloch after that date, where she was placed under Care and Maintenance. She was reduced to Category 'C' Reserve on 28.5.45 and was finally scrapped at Troon by the West of Scotland Shipbreaking Co Ltd during 2.46.

GROVE (L77)

GROVE worked up at Scapa and made passage to Alexandria via the Cape as part of the escort of Convoy WS17 which sailed from the Clyde on 22.3.42. On 27.3.42, GROVE, with LEAMINGTON, ALDENHAM and VOLUNTEER, sank U587 which had attacked the convoy. GROVE finally arrived at Alexandria on 18.5.42. Her active career with the 22nd Destroyer Flotilla at Alexandria lasted 24 days before her loss.

GROVE and TETCOTT sailed from Tobruk to Alexandria at 0000 hours on 12.6.42 but GROVE touched ground briefly at 0124 hours causing damage to her port propeller and shaft and this reduced her speed to $8\frac{1}{2}$ knots. At 0654 hours at position 32 35 N 25 30 E she was struck by two torpedoes from U77. These blew off her bow and stern, and she sank in 14 minutes. Although the torpedoes were sighted and the helm altered, she did not respond quickly enough at her slow speed. Six officers (including her CO) and 73 ratings escaped in GROVE's boats and were picked up by TETCOTT.

HAMBLEDON (L37)

HAMBLEDON's work-up, although started at Portland, was completed at Scapa which was safer. In 7.40 she was allocated to the 21st Destroyer Flotilla at Sheerness. However, on 7.10.40 HAMBLEDON triggered an acoustic mine off Dover and was heavily damaged. The hull plating and internal structure abaft the cut-up was severely damaged and the port and starboard 'A' brackets were fractured. The after-end immediately flooded and the vessel could not be steered. One crew member was lost and two injured.

HAMBLEDON was under repair at Chatham from 8.10.40 to 14.5.41 when she was allocated to the 16th Destroyer Flotilla at Harwich, where she served until transferred to the Mediterranean Fleet and the 58th Destroyer Division in 6.43. She had previously been detached to cover the 'Torch' landings in 11.42, being slightly damaged by the blast of a torpedo explosion on the 12th of that month. In her 11 months with the 58th Destroyer Division, her chief claim to fame was to escort the Support Force East for the Sicily landings, acting as Admiral Cunningham's HQ ship at Malta for the Salerno landings on 9.9.43. HAMBLEDON, with the destroyers TUMULT, BLENCATHRA and LAFOREY, sank U223 north of Sicily on 29.3.44.

She returned to Home Waters for the Normandy Landings and spent the last nine months of the war with the 16th Destroyer Flotilla. Her final action was to engage German MTB's off Flushing on the night of 12-13.4.45.

HAMBLEDON shown cocooned whilst in reserve at Harwich
(W.S.P.L.)

After acting as a local escort at Sheerness for seven months, HAMBLEDON reduced to reserve in December 1945. She was to remain in reserve for the next ten years — in Category 'B' Reserve at Harwich between 1946/8 and then Category 'C' Reserve until 1955, initially at Harwich and then at Barrow from 1953-54. HAMBLEDON was reduced to a hulk on 19.1.56 and subsequently handed over to BISCo on 2.8.57, being scrapped at Dunston on Tyne by Clayton & Davie.

HAYDON on completion 10.42. Note that the censor has blanked out her pendant number, radars and the background of the photograph. Compare with frontispiece.
(W.S.P.L.)

HAYDON (L75)

On completion of her work-up at Scapa, HAYDON operated in the Mediterranean for over two years until 12.44. Whilst in the Mediterranean she served with the 5th Destroyer Flotilla (from 12.42), 22nd Destroyer Flotilla (from 3.43), 59th Destroyer Division at Oran (from 6.43) and the 50th Escort Group (Algiers 9.43). She became an unattached vessel at Malta (in 12.43) and then joined the 18th Destroyer Flotilla at Malta for the whole of 1944. She was on escort duties for the landings at Sicily, Salerno and the South of France.

After returning to the UK, HAYDON operated with the 21st Destroyer Flotilla at Sheerness until the end of the war when she returned to Malta to refit for service in the Far East. She was lying at Malta when Japan surrendered in 9.45 and remained in the Mediterranean for the next two years, initially with the 3rd Destroyer Flotilla. HAYDON was damaged by fire and repaired at Malta between 7-9.47, and then returned to Chatham to refit for reserve before entering Category 'B' Reserve at Chatham for the next four years.

In 1951 she transferred to Sheerness for a year and was then laid up in a state of preservation at West Hartlepool until 1958. HAYDON was approved for scrapping on 18.3.58 and handed over to BISCo on 17.5.58. She arrived at Clayton & Davie's yard at Dunston on Tyne on 18.5.58 for scrapping.

HEYTHROP. Possibly the only photograph existing of this vessel. She is shown when newly completed in 1941
(N.M.M.)

HEYTHROP (L85)

On completion, HEYTHROP joined the Irish Sea Escort Force during 8.41 and immediately made passage to Gibraltar arriving there on 30.8.41. After repairing defects she escorted the damaged cruiser MANCHESTER and destroyer FIREDRAKE as far as 25° west before joining the 'Halberd' Convoy to Malta between 25.9. and 28.9.41. Off Cape Bon on 27.9.41 she rescued 300 survivors from the IMPERIAL STAR, previously sunk by an aircraft torpedo. HEYTHROP then escorted three empty supply ships from Malta to Gibraltar.

She then rounded the Cape and joined the 2nd Destroyer Flotilla at Alexandria on 15.11.41, immediately becoming part of the escort for Operation 'Aggressive' — the sending of reinforcements to Tobruk on 19.11.41. This operation was the first of several passages from Alexandria to Tobruk that HEYTHROP undertook between 11.41 and 2.42, generally under severe air attack. She escorted the supply ship ANTWERP from Alexandria (30.1.42) to Tobruk and returned to Alexandria (6.2.42). Between 12.2 and 16.2.42 HEYTHROP was part of the escort for convoy MW9A to Malta, and her final operation was to undertake an A/S sweep ahead of Convoy MG1 which sailed from Alexandria for Malta on 20.3.42.

When 40 miles north-east of Bardia, at position 32.20 N 25.28 E, HEYTHROP was hit 60 ft from the stern by a torpedo, fired at 1100 hours on 20.3.42 by U652. The ship was almost severed at No 3 mounting, which was blown overboard. The after portion of the ship was only connected by the starboard side plating and was flooding forward of bulkhead 105 by water gushing in around the top half of the port shaft gland plate. The ship was taken under tow, but at 1400 hours, the port gland plate fractured and the pumps could not cope with the inflow of water, especially after No 2 boiler failed. All hands, except for 15 lost in the initial explosion, were transferred to ERIDGE by boat and at 1615 hours the ship turned over on her starboard side and sank stern first.

HOLCOMBE (L56)

In 10.42, HOLCOMBE was allocated to the Mediterranean Fleet. On the 28th of that month she left the UK as part of the escort for convoy WS24, but was retained at Freetown as a convoy escort until 1.43. At that time she was re-allocated to the Western Mediterranean, leaving on 26.1.43 as escort for the aircraft carrier ILLUSTRIOUS which was en route to the UK. She joined the 59th Destroyer Division at Gibraltar on 1.2.43 and spent the next six months on escort duties around the North African ports. HOLCOMBE then joined the 56th Destroyer Division at Gibraltar (until 9.43) then the 46th Escort Group (at Algiers between 9-11.43) and finally the 'Mediterranean Hunts' at Malta. HOLCOMBE was on duty as an escort for Convoys KMS18, KMF18 and KMF19 during the invasion of Sicily and escorted the invasion fleet for Italy, subsequently escorting many convoys from North African ports to Malta, Taranto and Bari.

HOLCOMBE on completion. She survived barely a year, being torpedoed by U593 off the Algerian coast on 12.12.43, sinking in four minutes and 19 seconds with the loss of 84 lives   *(N.H.B. 10.42)*

On 12.12.43, whilst escorting convoy KMS34 off the Algerian coast, HOLCOMBE's sister ship TYNEDALE was torpedoed and sunk by U593 at 0710 hours. The other escorts, HOLCOMBE, CALPE, USS NIBLACK, USS BENSON and USS WAINWRIGHT hunted the U-boat but HOLCOMBE was torpedoed by U593 during the hunt. She was hit by a Gnat torpedo aft near the oil fuel tanks which burst into flame. The ship settled rapidly by the stern, listed to port until on her beam ends and sank almost vertically with her bows in the air 4 minutes and 19 seconds after being struck (timed by NIBLACK). There were 80 survivors (including her Commanding Officer and six other officers) three officers (one died of wounds) and 81 men (ten died of wounds) were lost.

A war view of HOLDERNESS, showing the bow chaser to advantage. She served with the 21st Destroyer Flotilla at Sheerness for the whole of the war   *(Brownell Collection)*

HOLDERNESS (L48)

After her work-up, HOLDERNESS joined the 21st Destroyer Flotilla at Sheerness on 5.9.40, and was to remain with this Flotilla for the whole of the war, seeing no foreign service. Her duty was the demanding, unrelenting and unrewarding one of protecting the east coast convoys. During these years, she was damaged three times by mines: on 16.9.40 slightly, on 5.7.41 (which required a month's repair) and on 5.12.43 when 16 miles off Cromer when her hull was severely buckled and some flooding occurred. On this last occasion, HOLDERNESS had to be beached near Parkeston Quay and was under repair by Green & Silley Weir at Blackwall, London for six months.

The highlights of her career were when she escorted the battleship QUEEN ELIZABETH from Devonport to the Clyde on 11-12.12.40; when she destroyed a Ju88 in the Thames Estuary on 10.3.41; and when she was in action with German motor torpedo boats (MTBs) on the nights of 14-15.3.41 and 20.2.42. On the latter occasion she sank one and took 18 prisoners.

HOLDERNESS seen laid up with a sister at Barrow, prior to her disposal by scrapping on 20.11.56.

(Ken Royall)

HOLDERNESS entered Category 'B2' Reserve at Harwich on 20.5.46, reducing to Category 'C' Reserve in 1949 and Extended Reserve in 1953. After de-humidification at Liverpool, she was laid-up at Barrow, until 20.11.56 when she was towed to Preston to be scrapped by T. W. Ward.

HURSLEY (L84)/Greek KRITI

HURSLEY, although nominally part of the 2nd Destroyer Flotilla of the Eastern Fleet, was attached to the Mediterranean Fleet on 29.6.42. She later operated with the 5th Destroyer Flotilla, the 22nd Destroyer Flotilla from February 1943 and finally the 'Levant Hunts' between 11-12.43 until her transfer to the Royal Hellenic Navy.

During this period, HURSLEY was present at the bombardment of Abu Dabba on 29.8.42 when she was slightly damaged by air attack. She participated in the sinking of two submarines — the Italian NARVALO with the destroyer PAKENHAM on 14.1.43 and a month later on 19.2.43 with the destroyer ISIS, she sank U562 between Tripoli and Malta. HURSLEY was also present at the blockade of Cape Bon in 5.43, the Sicily Invasion and was finally engaged in the Aegean Campaign; sinking the German submarine chaser UJ2109 and damaging the transport TRAPANI on the night of 16-17.10.43.

She became the Royal Hellenic Navy's KRITI on 2.11.43 but still served with the 22nd Flotilla for another year at which time she became a member of the wholly Greek 12th Flotilla at Piraeus until the war's end. During this period she acted as an escort for the Anzio Landings and the Invasion of Southern France. With the destroyers KIMBERLEY and CATTERICK she raided Rhodes on 1.5.45.

KRITI served on loan with the Greeks until being officially discarded on 12.12.59 when she returned to British ownership. On 27.4.60, however, she was sold for breaking up in Greece.

HURWORTH, after surviving the disasters of 1942, was lost by mining off Calini island in the Aegean on 22.10.43 with heavy loss of life *(Brownell Collection)*

HURWORTH (L28)

In 11.41, HURWORTH sailed as part of the escort for Convoy WS14 for the Cape but was retained at Freetown for two months on local escort duties. She did not join the 5th Destroyer Flotilla at Alexandria until 6.2.42, remaining with this Flotilla until 7.43 when she became leader of the 22nd Destroyer Flotilla until her loss.

HURWORTH's period in the Mediterranean was one of hectic activity as within days of joining the Flotilla she covered FARNDALE's return to Alexandria, had escorted Convoy MW9B and participated in the first Battle of Sirte. A month later, HURWORTH was one of the close escorts for another Malta Convoy; escorting the damaged transport BRECONSHIRE into Marsaxlokk Bay on 25.3.42. April and May 1942 saw her escorting convoys to Tobruk and with ERIDGE and the destroyer HERO, she sank U568 off Sollum on 28.5.42.

June 1942 saw her as part of the escort for the unsuccessful 'Vigorous' Convoy to Malta. A month later she bombarded Mersa Matruh on three occasions and during 9.42 she took part in the disastrous commando raid on Tobruk, rescuing survivors of the destroyer ZULU. Finally on 30.10.42 HURWORTH, with DULVERTON, PETARD and PAKENHAM and aided by aircraft, sank U559 40 miles off Port Said. This occurred at a time when HURWORTH was on local escort duties in the Levant.

On 20.11.42 she was one of the escorts of the convoy that relieved the siege of Malta and between then and June 1943 she made two passages per month between Alexandria and Malta.

After appearing on escort duties in the assault phases of the Sicily Landings, HURWORTH then protected the transport anchorages. She was then directed to the Aegean in 9.43 whilst on escort duties between Malta and Haifa. On 17.9.43 with CROOME, she landed two companies of infantry at Leros to prevent its seizure by the Germans. For the next month she undertook sweeps against enemy shipping and the bombardment of enemy held islands. However, on a supply mission to Leros on 22.10.43 with the Greek destroyer ADRIAS (qv) she ran onto a newly laid minefield east of Calini Island. ADRIAS lost her bow and was beached in Turkish waters, whilst HURWORTH broke in two; both parts sinking within 15 minutes in position 36.59 N 27.06 E. Eighty five officers and men were rescued and taken to Turkey.

KANARIS had originally been launched as HATHERLEIGH, prior to her transfer to the Royal Hellenic Navy during 3.42 *(N.H.B.)*

Greek KANARIS (ex HATHERLEIGH) (L53)

On 24.3.42 before completion HATHERLEIGH together with MODBURY was transferred to the Royal Hellenic Navy. After completing her work-up at Scapa, KANARIS' first duty on 1.9.42 was to escort her damaged sister ADRIAS to the Tyne for repairs. She then returned to Scapa as escort with BLEAN and

PUCKERIDGE, for the aircraft carrier FURIOUS. In company with PUCKERIDGE she joined the escort for Convoy WS23 for Durban on 30.9.42. KANARIS was to spend the remainder of the war in the Mediterranean, with the 22nd Destroyer Flotilla (to 11.43), the 5th Destroyer Flotilla (to 7.44), the 57th Destroyer Division (to 12.44). After service with the Aegean Escort Flotilla, she was by 5.45 with the wholly Greek 12th Destroyer Flotilla.

KANARIS spent most of the war on escort duties, especially convoys to Malta in early 1943 but was present at the blockade of Cape Bon and the invasion of Sicily where with the destroyers ESKIMO and EXMOOR she attempted to enter Augusta but was beaten off by accurate coastal battery fire. Further convoy duties followed the invasion of Italy but on 19.3.44 she was damaged in collision with the cruiser HAWKINS and was under repair at Massawa until 8.44. Duties with the British Aegean Force followed in the autumn of 1944 and this was followed by further escort duties and duties against Greek E.L.A.S. terrorists until the end of the war.

KANARIS was in service with the Royal Hellenic Navy until 12.12.59 when she was officially discarded and later scrapped in Greece.

The Polish KRAKOWIAK pictured in 12.42, whilst serving with the 15th Destroyer Flotilla at Portsmouth
(N.H.B.)

KRAKOWIAK/SILVERTON (L115)

It was agreed on 3.4.41, that SILVERTON and OAKLEY (1) were to be taken over by the Polish Navy to replace the ex-French destroyer OURAGAN then operated by the Poles. On completion KRAKOWIAK was allocated to the 15th Destroyer Flotilla at Plymouth and served with this unit until 6.43.

Between 22.12.41 and 1.11.42 she formed part of the escort for the raiding force for the Lofoten Islands. On 17.6.42, KRAKOWIAK with the destroyers WILD SWAN and BEAGLE and the frigate SPEY were part of the support group sent to aid convoy HG84. The group was itself attacked by aircraft and WILD SWAN was lost. Four months later KRAKOWIAK with FERNIE, TYNEDALE and BROCKLESBY was in action against German torpedo boats near Cap de la Hague on the night of 13-14.10.42 and again whilst protecting a convoy off Start Point on 5.5.43 she drove off attacking MTBs.

In 6.43, KRAKOWIAK sailed for the Mediterranean where she stayed for the next ten months as a unit of the Gibraltar Escort Force, the 60th Destroyer Division (to 9.43), the 48th Escort Group (until 11.43), the Mediterranean Hunts (between 11-12.43) and finally the 18th Destroyer Flotilla. During this period, she acted as an escort for the invasion of Italy; shelled Calino with PETARD and ROCKWOOD on 11.11.43 and 17 days later attended the cruiser BIRMINGHAM after she had been torpedoed on passage from Gibraltar to the Levant.

After returning to the UK, KRAKOWIAK spent until 8.44 as an unattached vessel on invasion duties, based at Portsmouth. She had engaged, with GLAISDALE and URSA, the German torpedo-boats T28, MOWE and JAGUAR on the night of 9-10.6.44. KRAKOWIAK then joined the 16th Destroyer Flotilla and served in home waters until being paid off into reserve on 23.7.46 when her loan to the Poles was terminated. She was officially returned to the Royal Navy on 25.9.46 and as SILVERTON was laid up in Category 'B' Reserve at Harwich, three days later. SILVERTON remained in reserve for the next 13 years (1947-9 Category 'B2' Reserve at Harwich, 1949-1952 Category 'C' at Harwich, 1952-3 at Sheerness and finally Class II Reserve at Chatham). SILVERTON was a representative of the Reserve Fleet at the Coronation Review. She was approved for scrapping on 11.3.58; allocated to BISCo and towed to Ward's Grays yard on 11.3.59. The net scrap realisation was £17,400.

Believed to be the only existing photograph of the Polish KUJAWIAK taken prior to her loss off Malta on 16.6.42
(Polish Naval Association)

KUJAWIAK (ex OAKLEY (I)) (L72)

On 3.4.41 it was agreed that OAKLEY (1) and SILVERTON were to be taken over by the Polish Navy, on completion, in place of OURAGAN which had been taken over by the Free French.

Whilst working up on 18.6.41 KUJAWIAK was attacked by German aircraft with machine guns which caused the explosion of a 4" ready use locker. On completion of her work-up she joined the 15th Destroyer Flotilla at Plymouth on escort and patrol duties until her Mediterranean service. The highlight of her career with the 15th Flotilla was her participation as part of the raiding force for the Lofoten Raid between 22.12.41 and 1.1.42.

KUJAWIAK was despatched to the Mediterranean in 6.42 as part of the escort for the 'Harpoon' Convoy from Gibraltar to Malta. The convoy which included the freighters TROILUS, BURDWAN, TANIMBAR, ORARI and the tanker KENTUCKY, escorted by the cruisers LIVERPOOL and CAIRO, the destroyers BEDOUIN, MARNE, MATCHLESS, ITHURIEL, PARTRIDGE, BLANKNEY, MIDDLETON, BADSWORTH and the minesweepers HEBE, SPEEDY, RYE and HYTHE. After several days of severe sea and air attack, during which the merchant ships TANIMBAR, BURDWAN and KENTUCKY and the destroyer BEDOUIN were sunk, the remnants of the convoy reached Valletta Harbour. However, on the 16th KUJAWIAK was mined and sunk off Valletta and the destroyers BADSWORTH (qv), MATCHLESS, the minesweeper HEBE and the freighter ORARI were damaged on the same minefield.

The final destroyer lost in European waters. LA COMBATTANTE, originally named HALDON, was transferred to the Free French during 12.42   *(N.H.B. 2.43)*

LA COMBATTANTE (ex HALDON) (L19)

HALDON was damaged by bombing on the night of 13-14.3.41, whilst on the slipway at Fairfield's. On 1.12.42 she was taken over by the Free French and commissioned as LA COMBATTANTE a fortnight later. After working up at Scapa she joined the First Destroyer Flotilla at Portsmouth until late 1944. LA COMBATTANTE was to be involved in many actions during this period.

On 7.10.43 she was engaged by shore batteries whilst patrolling the Le Havre/Cap Barfleur area. She sank two German MTBs, both off Selsey Bill — S147 on 25.4.44 and S141 on the night of 12-13.5.44. Unfortunately 15 days later, on 28.5.44, she sank the British MTB732 in error.

On 'D' Day LA COMBATTANTE was part of the Support Force for 'Juno' Beach and eight days later General de Gaulle visited the Eastern Assault Area aboard her. Further patrol and escort duties followed off the invasion beaches with LA COMBATTANTE being attacked by an MTB on the night of 7-8.7.44; suffering collision damage on 21.7.44 and participating in an attack on an enemy convoy off Cap d'Antifer on 28.8.44 with MTBs 253, 254 and 257 in which several vessels were sunk.

On 19.12.44 LA COMBATTANTE rescued the survivors of SS STEEL TRAVELER (mined and sunk at 1700 hours on 18.12.44).

LA COMBATTANTE joined the 21st Destroyer Flotilla during 12.44, but her career with this unit was to be brief, as at 2345 hours on 23.2.45 she blew up off the East Dudgeon Buoy. 118 survivors were rescued by MTBs 763 and 770 but 66 of her crew died. (Mines had been laid in that area by the German 2nd and 5th 'S' boat Flotillas on the night of 17-18.2.45, but others have claimed that LA COMBATTANTE was lost by small boat attack).

LAMERTON (L88)

After work-up LAMERTON served initially in the Western Approaches Command. On 25.10.41 whilst escorting Convoy HG74 she sank the Italian submarine GALILEO FERRARIS after a long gun duel. In 12.41, she was attached to the Home Fleet and then joined the 6th Destroyer Flotilla in 3.42 for three months. During this period LAMERTON was involved in several notable actions — the Lofoten raid, anti-shipping raids along the Norwegian coast during January 1942 and escort duties with Russian Convoys PQ13, PQ14, PQ15 and PQ16; attacking but not sinking a U-boat in the Norwegian Sea whilst escorting PQ13. Under refit at the time of the ill-fated PQ17 Operation, LAMERTON was allocated to the Mediterranean Fleet in 7.42 but was damaged in a collision whilst escorting a troop convoy WS27 on 31.7.42 and was under repair at Liverpool until 26.9.42 not joining the 57th Destroyer Division of the Mediterranean Fleet until 11.42.

She was to spend the next two years with the 57th Division and was involved initially in the 'Torch' operations, covering the Algiers Landings on 7.11.42, the paratroop assault at Bougie on 10.11.42 and the Commando landing for the seizure of Bone two days later. During the first five months of 1943, LAMERTON was part of the inshore squadron. Between the 20th and 23rd of February, with BICESTER, WILTON and later WHEATLAND and RAF aircraft she hunted and finally sank U443 after a hunt lasting 63 hours. The blockade of Cape Bon in 5.43 was quickly followed by LAMERTON providing gunfire support for the Sicily Landings and acting as an escort for the Salerno landings (9.9.43).

LAMERTON survived the war and was transferred to the Indian Navy as GOMATI in 4.53

(Brownell Collection)

In October 1943 LAMERTON undertook two patrols and a supply mission to Leros, but was at Malta when Leros was recaptured. She spent the next 14 months on convoy escort, patrol duties and coastal bombardment duties on the west coast of Italy and in the Adriatic. A spell of duty in Greek waters during 12.44 was followed by LAMERTON's transfer to the 5th Destroyer Flotilla until 3.45, when she was recalled to the UK for service with the 16th Destroyer Flotilla at Harwich on coastal escort duties until the war's end.

LAMERTON was one of the vessels allocated to the 18th Flotilla at Trincomalee sailing for Simonstown to refit during 7.45 and that is where she was on VJ Day.

She returned to the UK in 12.45 and paid off into Category 'B' Reserve at Harwich on 20.3.46. She was relegated to Category 'B2' Reserve a year later and was to remain at Harwich until 1952.

On 27.4.53 LAMERTON was transferred on loan to India as GOMATI, being purchased outright five years later. GOMATI served as a training vessel for many years, finally paying-off during 1975 and was then stricken from the effective list.

LAUDERDALE, seen on the day of her commissioning 24.12.41, was the only Hunt to cross the Atlantic for trials with the Royal Canadian Navy during 2.42

(N.M.M.)

LAUDERDALE (L95)

LAUDERDALE joined the Western Approaches Command and the 20th Escort Group briefly in early 1942, but on 16.2.42 she sailed from Londonderry accompanied by the destroyer CALDWELL on being allocated to the Western Local Escort Force at St Johns, Newfoundland. She arrived at St Johns on 21.2.42 and Halifax three days later. LAUDERDALE then acted as a local escort between Halifax and St Johns for the next month, escorting convoys SC72, ON70 and SC75 during that period. It is assumed that LAUDERDALE was under trial by the Royal Canadian Navy as an alternative to the pre-war destroyers and TOWN Class vessels then on loan to the RCN. Nothing came of this trial; the Hunts were probably rejected because of their lack of endurance. LAUDERDALE's trip is the only recorded voyage of a Hunt across the Atlantic.

She returned to Londonderry on 30.3.42 and after a further period with the Western Approaches Command she transferred on patrol and escort duties to the Rosyth Escort Force until 2.43. After refitting at Hull between 2-3.43, LAUDERDALE made passage to the Mediterranean where she was allocated to the 60th Destroyer Division at Malta until mid 1944. She participated in the blockade of Cape Bon in 5.43, the invasion of Sicily and the invasion of the South of France in 8.44. By this time LAUDERDALE had joined the 5th Destroyer Flotilla at Alexandria with which she served until the war's end.

After briefly returning to the UK to give leave, LAUDERDALE was on passage to refit at Simonstown when the Japanese war ended. However, the refit proceeded and on its completion in 1.46, she returned to the Mediterranean.

LAUDERDALE was surveyed during 3.46 and was transferred on loan to the Royal Hellenic Navy on 5.5.46 as the AIGAION. She was to serve with the Greeks until 22.9.59 when approval was given to dispose of her locally and she was finally discarded by the Greeks on 12.12.59.

LEDBURY at her launch on 27.9.41. Compare her hull with that of BRISSENDEN   (N.M.M.)

LEDBURY (L90)
LEDBURY's construction was delayed by bomb damage during air raids on the Thornycroft yard. She worked up at Scapa during February and March 1942 when she joined the 8th Destroyer Flotilla, Home Fleet and was engaged in escorting major warships and auxiliaries between Scapa Flow and Iceland until 6.42. Between 27.6.42 and 4.7.42 LEDBURY was part of the ocean escort for the ill-fated convoy PQ17 from Iceland until the convoy was scattered on 4.7.42 and almost completely destroyed.

A month later, LEDBURY with DERWENT and BRAMHAM formed part of the close escort for the 'Pedestal' convoy operation to Malta, and she played a major part with PENN and BRAMHAM in escorting the damaged tanker OHIO into Malta on 13.8.42. After repairing at Grimsby between 8.9.42 and 7.10.42, she joined the Shetland and Orkneys Command and continued her escort duties between Iceland and the Orkneys until 3.43 when she started a refit at Sheerness which lasted until 25.5.43.

LEDBURY is seen here in 5.43 prior to her transfer to the Mediterranean after strenuous service on Arctic convoys in the previous year.   *(N.H.B.)*

LEDBURY then joined the Mediterranean Fleet as an escort in 6.43 and served with the 57th Destroyer Division (7-8.43), the 58th Destroyer Division (8-9.43), and the 59th Destroyer Division until the end of the war. During this period she was in attendance at the invasions of Sicily and Italy, shelled Durazzo with BLACKMORE on the night of 15-16.1.44 and covered the return of British troops to Athens in October 1944 in addition to her usual escort duties.

LEDBURY returned briefly to the UK in 5.45 and refitted at Gibraltar between 6.45 and 1.46. She returned to the UK and entered reserve at Portsmouth during 3.46. She was to languish in reserve at Portsmouth until scrapped in 7.58 (LEDBURY was in Category 'B' Reserve until 1947, Category 'B2' Reserve between 1947/49, Category 'C' 1949/52 and after a refit, Category 1 Reserve 1952/55 and finally Extended Reserve). She was delivered to Shipbreaking Industries at Charlestown, Fife on 12.5.58, but was transferred to their nearby Rosyth yard for demolition during 7.58.

LIDDESDALE in the Firth of Forth on 3.8.42. Note the standard feature of Hunts used on east coast convoys — the 2pdr bow-chaser   *(N.H.B.)*

LIDDESDALE (L100)

On completion LIDDESDALE joined the Rosyth Escort Force and was engaged on east coast convoy work for the next two years. Apart from a minor collision with the west jetty at Rosyth during 8.42, these years were comparatively uneventful for LIDDESDALE. She seems however to have suffered a lot of minor defects during this period.

LIDDESDALE was allocated to the Mediterranean Fleet in 3.43 and served with the following units; the 56th Destroyer Division at Gibraltar (to 9.43), the 46th Escort Group at Algiers (to 11.43), the 59th Destroyer Division at Malta (to 12.44) and finally the 22nd Destroyer Flotilla until the end of the war. LIDDESDALE's greatest achievement, with the support of the destroyers TENACIOUS and TERMAGANT, was to sink U453 north-east of Cape Spartivento on 21.5.44. She was damaged by shore batteries (three hits) whilst attacking shipping in Pegadia Bay, Scarpanto on 28.9.44 and was out of action for 17 days.

LIDDESDALE also undertook escort duties at the invasions of Sicily, Italy and the South of France and was part of the British Aegean Force freeing the Aegean Islands in 10.44. In 7.45 she was part of the 3rd Destroyer Flotilla of the Mediterranean Fleet but did not remain long on station, as she returned to the UK later in the year and reduced to Category 'B' Reserve at Chatham on 11.12.45.

LIDDESDALE remained in reserve at Chatham in 1946/7 and at Harwich in 1947/8 by which time she was made available for disposal as her condition was poor. On 1.10.48 LIDDESDALE was towed from Harwich bound for the Tyne for scrapping by J. J. King at Gateshead.

LIMBOURNE shortly after completion in 12.42 *(N.H.B.)*

LIMBOURNE (L57)

LIMBOURNE was very active in her one year of existence. While working up in 11.42 she escorted the battleship HOWE to the Mediterranean and returned to the UK as escort for the DUKE OF YORK and VICTORIOUS. LIMBOURNE then joined the 15th Destroyer Flotilla at Plymouth, where she remained for the rest of her career.

In January and February 1943 LIMBOURNE was to be found escorting convoys to Gibraltar and North Africa, and following a month in dockyard hands at Portsmouth to fit a new propeller, she escorted the French battleship COURBET to the Clyde. The next five months of her career were spent on sweeps off the French coast, protecting light forces and undertaking anti-submarine patrols in the Bay of Biscay. On 4.10.43, north of Morlaix, LIMBOURNE received slight damage in action with enemy destroyers.

A second view of LIMBOURNE. She was to survive barely a year, being lost with the cruiser CHARYBDIS in a disastrous action with German torpedo boats off the Channel Islands on 23.10.43 *(Brownell Collection)*

LIMBOURNE was lost on 23.10.43 off the Channel Islands in the same disastrous action that saw the cruiser CHARYBDIS sunk by torpedoes from the German torpedo boats T23 and T27. At the time CHARYBDIS with the other units of Force X — the destroyers LIMBOURNE, GRENVILLE, ROCKET, WENSLEYDALE, TALYBONT and STEVENSTONE, were attempting to intercept the blockade runner MUNSTERLAND.

LIMBOURNE herself was torpedoed forward by T22. All the fore-end structure below the waterline, from just forward of the boiler rooms and the forecastle deck forward of the bridge was blown away. She was taken in tow, but yawed badly and was finally sunk by torpedoes from TALYBONT and ROCKET. One officer and 41 ratings were lost.

A fine view of MELBREAK taken in 7.43   (N.H.B.)

MELBREAK (L73)

MELBREAK was to spend until 2.45 with the 15th Destroyer Flotilla at Plymouth, before joining the 21st Flotilla at Sheerness until the end of the war. Whilst with the 15th Flotilla, MELBREAK had several deployments off station, notably escorting convoys to and from Gibraltar in 12.42; and escorting the ILLUSTRIOUS, RENOWN and FURIOUS to the Clyde, where she arrived on 4.2.43. In 6.43, she carried combined services personnel and equipment to Gibraltar, Malta and Casablanca, leaving Gibraltar for the UK with Convoy XK9 on 22.6.43.

MELBREAK also had several engagements with enemy MTB's and patrol craft, the first of which was on the night of 9-10.7.43 when in company with WENSLEYDALE and GLAISDALE she engaged a convoy off Ushant. This was escorted by the German minesweepers M9, M10, M12, M84 and M135, of which the last named was sunk. MELBREAK received considerable damage in this action and was repairing damage and being refitted at London until 2.9.43. She was again in action on 15.3.44 whilst protecting convoy WP492 off Lands End against the attacks of the German 5th and 9th MTB Flotillas.

After operating as part of Force 'O' for the landings on Omaha Beach, which she bombarded, MELBREAK was to be a participant in four actions during the next few months. Five days after 'D' Day she was indecisively engaged by MTB's off Cap d'Antifer.

On the night of 21-22.7.44 MELBREAK was in action against MTBs S132, S90, S135 and the torpedo boat T28 between Boulogne and Le Havre. A month later, on the night of 20-21.8.44 MELBREAK with WATCHMAN and FORESTER drove off the German 8th MTB Flotilla whilst on convoy duty off Beachy Head. Three nights later, MELBREAK with the frigate RETALICK and MTBs 205, 208 and 212 attacked the retreating German ships off Cap d'Antifer and Fecamp. MELBREAK received superficial damage.

MELBREAK was not to be so lucky a few days later when on patrol on 28.8.44 she was bombed by an unknown aircraft and sustained moderate flooding forward and reported five dead and 15 wounded. She was under repair and refit at Barry until 4.11.44.

The day before VE Day MELBREAK ran aground and received damage to her A/S dome, her keel plates were also pierced and badly distorted between the dome and the forward magazine. MELBREAK was under repair at Sheerness until 11.8.45.

MELBREAK, pictured here in 6.53, as a representative of the Reserve Fleet at the Coronation Review. Note the changed pendant number *(W.S.P.L.)*

MELBREAK was never to re-commission, being in reserve at Chatham until 22.11.56 when she arrived at Grays and was scrapped by Ward's. However, one bright spot in her post-war career was her appearance at the Coronation Review in 6.53 as a representative of the Reserve Fleet.

MENDIP (L60)

MENDIP's career in the Royal Navy was conventional but after the war she was to see service in no less than three different Navies!

MENDIP shortly after the depth charge explosion at Scapa on 24.10.40 during her work-up *(N.M.M.)*

MENDIP had only been working up a week at Scapa, when an explosion of her own depth charges on 24.10.40 caused severe damage, with her steering gear being blown away. On 11.11.40 MENDIP left Scapa in tow of the tug CHAMPION for repairs at Smith's Dock that were not completed until 17.2.41.

After successfully working-up MENDIP joined the 21st Destroyer Flotilla escorting east coast convoys and North Sea patrols until her transfer to the Mediterranean in 6.43. Highlights of this active portion of her career included being attacked by aircraft whilst escorting convoy FS449 on 30.3.41 and escorting the minelayer TEVIOTBANK when laying mines as part of the East Coast Barrage on 20.6.41. A day later she picked up nine survivors from the Dutch freighter SCHIELAND which had been bombed and sunk while with the Convoy FS520. She bombarded Dieppe with CATTISTOCK and QUORN on 26.7.41 and with barrage fire frustrated four separate low level bombing attacks on Convoy FS605 on 17.9.41. Sixteen days later she fought off an MTB attack on convoy FS615.

On the night of 19-20.2.42, MENDIP had a lucky escape when a torpedo passed down the port side of the vessel during an action with MTBs whilst protecting convoy FS29. Finally on the night of 24-25.1.43, in company with the destroyer WINDSOR she drove off the S boats of the German 2nd, 4th and 6th Flotillas which attacked the convoy they were escorting.

This and the next photograph show the extent of the damage to MENDIP, when docked at Smith's Dock on 15.11.40. Note that the rudder is missing, as is the steering gear, but the propellers appear undamaged and the two 4" guns have been removed from their mounts. Repairs took four months *(N.M.M.)*

After a short refit at Chatham between 19.5-9.6.43 MENDIP formed part of the escort of Convoy KM17 for Bone and then escorted Convoy KM18 to the Sicily Assault Area on 10.7.43. MENDIP gave gunfire support at the Salerno Landings on 9.9.43 before returning to Malta for repairs and then joined the 58th Destroyer Division until 5.44 when she returned to the UK. During this period MENDIP carried out supporting patrols and covered convoys around the Italian coast. With the destroyers ILEX and NUBIAN, she bombarded the north bank of the Garigliano river on 23.11.43.

After carrying out escort duties to the American beaches at Normandy until 7.44, she refitted at Liverpool between 1.8.44 and 22.10.44 before rejoining the 21st Flotilla for the remainder of the war.

She reduced to reserve at Harwich on 20.5.45 and remained there until 12.47 when she was transferred on loan to Nationalist China for five years. She recommissioned a month later on 21.1.48, but was not renamed LIN FU until her arrival in the Far East on 19.5.48. The defeat of the Nationalist forces meant that LIN FU was returned to the Royal Navy at Hong Kong on 29.5.49 and reverted to her original name.

On 9.6.49 MENDIP sailed for Singapore where she remained in commission for three months covering the refit of the destroyer CONSORT. She thus became the only Hunt to see active service in the Far East after the end of the war.

MENDIP pictured during 1.48 after recommissioning for service with the Chinese Nationalists. She was not renamed LIN FU until after her arrival in the Far East in 5.48. She served as LIN FU for a year until reverting to the Royal Navy   *(Wright & Logan)*

MENDIP paid off at Singapore on 12.9.49, but over the next two months sailed via Colombo and Aden to arrive at Alexandria on 9.11.49. Six days later she was transferred to the Royal Egyptian Navy and renamed MOHAMED ALI. Two years later she was renamed IBRAHIM EL AWAL.

MENDIP as the Egyptian IBRAHIM EL AWAL in 1951   *(W.S.P.L.)*

On 31.10.56 the IBRAHIM EL AWAL was captured off Haifa by Israeli Forces and incorporated into the Israeli Navy as the HAIFA in 1.57. The HAIFA was to undertake training duties with the Israelis for many years and was then discarded in 1972 after two years service as a hulk.

MEYNELL on 23.12.41, after a year's service with the 21st Destroyer Flotilla. She shows few changes in equipment from when she first commissioned, except the bow-chaser   *(N.H.B.)*

MEYNELL (L82)

As a member of the 21st Destroyer Flotilla for the whole of the war, MEYNELL had a career of unspectacular and arduous work as an escort for the east coast convoys. However, she managed the occasional excursion to other stations, especially between 15.2. and 14.3.43 when she escorted Convoy JW53 to north Russia and returned with Convoy RA53.

Her only action of note was on the night of 25-26.2.44 when she engaged vessels of the German 8th MTB Flotilla. MEYNELL served off Normandy after the landings, and suffered damage when she grounded on 31.10.44. Repairs on the Thames to her starboard shaft, propeller and 'A' bracket were not completed until 14.3.45.

From 11.9.45, her armament was stripped at Rosyth on her conversion to an aircraft target ship. After a period of service in the Mediterranean, MEYNELL had reduced to Category 'B' Reserve at Harwich by 12.46 and remained there until 1949, when she reduced to Category 'C' Reserve, also at Harwich until 1952. In this year she transferred to Sheerness and a year later moved again to Barrow where she was laid up in Class III Reserve.

Two further views of MEYNELL, the top picture shows her configuration as a disarmed aircraft target ship between 9.45-12.46. The bottom picture, taken on 18.4.53, shows her laid up in Devonshire Basin at Barrow, still disarmed and looking a sorry sight *(Top W.S.P.L. Kennedy. Bottom Ken Royall)*

MEYNELL, after transfer and refit, as the Ecuadorian PRESIDENTE VELASCO IBARRA in 1955
(W.S.P.L. Kennedy)

On 18.10.54 she was transferred to Ecuador and renamed PRESIDENTE VELASCO IBARRA but did not finally commission into the Ecuadorian Navy until 8.55 after being refitted by White's at Cowes. She was to serve Ecuador for over 20 years until stricken from service on 5.5.78.

R.H.N. MIAOULIS formerly MODBURY. The shot was taken on 16.11.42 as she left her builders Swan Hunters for her work-up at Scapa, as she did not commission until 11.12.42   *(N.H.B.)*

Greek MIAOULIS (ex MODBURY) (L91)

On 24.3.42 permission was given to allocate MODBURY to the Royal Hellenic Navy and she was commissioned as MIAOULIS on 11.12.42. After working up at Scapa until 1.43, she joined the combined Convoy WS26/KMF8 from the Clyde on 22.1.43 returning to Londonderry a week later after escorting the convoy to the limit of her endurance. At Londonderry, some personnel were changed due to ill-feeling between the Greek and British members of her crew. The British contingent consisted of liaison and signals staff.

After escorting the Convoy KMF9 to Gibraltar, where she arrived on 12.2.43, MIAOULIS stayed at Gibraltar undertaking extensive A/S exercises before passage to the eastern Mediterranean and her duties with the 5th Flotilla. She was to serve with this Flotilla until 7.44 when she joined the Greek Flotilla until the end of the war. She was engaged in the Sicily and Italy Landings before becoming heavily embroiled in the Aegean Campaign in 10.43. MIAOULIS, in company with the cruisers PENELOPE and SIRIUS, attacked an enemy convoy off Stampalia on 7.10.43. Ten days later with HURSLEY she sank the submarine chaser UJ2109 (ex

British WIDNES), the transport TRAPANI (1,855 tons) and two other vessels. On 18.10.43, she bombarded Kos with HURSLEY and then undertook two supply missions to Leros on the nights of 20-21.10.43 and 26-27.10.43. On the night of 5-6.11.43 she bombarded Kos and then Rhodes before returning to the Gulf of Kos.

MIAOULIS was to remain in the eastern Mediterranean until the end of the war, being part of the British Aegean Force re-occupying the Aegean Islands between 24.9. and 31.10.44. She remained with the Royal Hellenic Navy until 23.9.60 when she returned to UK control but was sold locally on 19.7.61 and scrapped in Greece.

MIDDLETON saw arduous service in Arctic waters until 2.44, when she was the last Hunt in service with the Home Fleet   (N.H.B.)

MIDDLETON (L74)

MIDDLETON's work-up was interrupted by the need to provide an AA escort for convoy PQ11 to Russia. After completing her work-up she joined the 17th Destroyer Flotilla of the Home Fleet escorting Russian convoys but seeing little action until 6.42. On the fifth of that month, she sailed as part of the escort for the 'Harpoon' convoy supplying materials to Malta. After refuelling at Gibraltar, the escort passed through the Straits of Gibraltar on the night of 11-12.6.42. The next four days were ones of savage surface, air and submarine attack, the convoy losing four out of its six merchant ships and the destroyers BEDOUIN and KUJAWIAK (qv), whilst the cruiser LIVERPOOL was severely damaged and returned to Gibraltar. MIDDLETON survived unscathed and returned to Gibraltar as escort for the cruiser CALCUTTA.

She then returned to Home Fleet duties and was one of the escorts for the covering force for the ill-fated PQ17 convoy. MIDDLETON was to return to Murmansk on 2.8.42, with her sister BLANKNEY and the fleet destroyers MARTIN and MARNE, carrying ammunition and supplies for those vessels of Convoy PQ17 that had reached Russia. She remained at Murmansk until 13.9.42 when she formed part of the escort for Convoy QP14 which arrived home with the loss of three merchant ships and two escorts to U-boats attack. MIDDLETON arrived at Scapa on 26.9.42 after an absence of two months. She had attacked U-boat contacts on three occasions on 20th, 21st and 22nd of September but without result. MIDDLETON resumed her escort duties with the Home Fleet until 11.42, and was then ordered to provide an additional escort for QP15 but the convoy had scattered in the prevailing bad weather.

After a refit at Hull between 3.12.42 and 4.1.43, MIDDLETON undertook escort duties between the UK and Iceland until 2.44. Refitted at Bristol between 10.3.44 and 7.4.44, she was subsequently attached to the Portsmouth Command for the Normandy Landings. On 6.6.44 she escorted the 15th Minesweeping Flotilla to the beaches as part of Force 'S'. MIDDLETON then remained in the area and assisted the army by bombardments and later aided A/S and AA patrols. During this period, accompanied by a Flotilla of MTBs she attacked a German convoy of eight landing craft off Cap d'Antifer on 28.8.44 sinking four of them. Nine days later MIDDLETON suffered her only damage, when hit by gunfire from the batteries at Cap Gris Nez. One member of her crew was killed. Like many of her sisters, MIDDLETON joined the 21st Flotilla at Sheerness during 9.44 remaining on station until 7.45 when she transferred to the East Indies Fleet. She sailed from Portsmouth on 14.7.45 for Simonstown to refit arriving there on 4.8.45. Her refit was completed on 29.12.45 when she sailed for Portsmouth and paid off into Category 'B' Reserve during 1.46.

She was to remain in reserve at Portsmouth until 1953 (Category 'B2' 1947/49, Category 'C' 1949/51, Category 'B' 1951/3) when she transferred to Class 2 Reserve at Penarth. MIDDLETON did not stay at Penarth long, as a year later she transferred to Gibraltar until 1955. In August that year, she was towed to Harwich where she was hulked as part of an artificial harbour.

MIDDLETON was handed over to BISCo in 8.57 arriving at Blyth on 4.10.57 for demolition by Hughes Bolckow on 4.10.57. In 2.58, BISCo reported that she had been totally broken up.

OAKLEY (II), originally to have been named TICKHAM, is pictured on commissioning in 5.42 after her completion was seriously delayed because of the bombing of Yarrow's yard *(N.H.B.)*

OAKLEY (II) (ex TICKHAM) (L98)

OAKLEY's completion was delayed by bombing of the shipyard. Defects that arose during her trials delayed her departure from Yarrow's until 22.6.42, when she sailed for Scapa. She was then immediately used as an escort for a decoy convoy for the ill-fated PQ17 Convoy before completing her ten day work-up. OAKLEY then undertook escort duties for convoys to and from the Faroes, as a unit of the Orkney and Shetland Command. This was followed by a period of detachment as escort for tankers at Lowe Sound, Spitzbergen during the PQ18 operation and in late November 1942 she escorted QP15 from Iceland to Scapa.

She then escorted Convoy KMF9 from Milford Haven to Algiers, joining the 59th Destroyer Division at Oran on 16.2.43. When engaged in operations off Cape Bon on 9.5.43, OAKLEY and BICESTER were mistakenly attacked by 18 Spitfires and BICESTER was left badly damaged. OAKLEY then participated in the invasion of Sicily; initially on gun-support duties and then on escort duties between Sousse and Sicily. She then undertook escort duties between Gibraltar, North Africa and Italy for the rest of the year. On 12.12.43 while entering Taranto, OAKLEY fouled a submerged wreck, sustaining considerable damage to her hull and propellers.

She did not complete repairs at Taranto until 4.44 and then she immediately started a refit which was completed a month later. She then rejoined the 59th Destroyer Division. Her duty was to escort part of the 'Dragoon' Convoy to the St Tropez invasion beaches on 12.8.44 and she continued to operate on convoy duties concerned with the invasion until 9.44. OAKLEY was then allocated at the end of September to cover minesweeping operations in the Gulf of Athens, and a month later was present at the occupation of Athens, despite communist opposition.

By 12.44, the major threats to merchant shipping in the Mediterranean had ended and OAKLEY, although allocated to the East Indies Fleet, was sent home to Chatham for modifications. She served briefly with the 21st Flotilla during 2.45, before beginning a month's refit at Portsmouth on 3.3.45. After working up, OAKLEY left to complete her refit at Taranto and was still refitting there on 3.9.45. She returned to Portsmouth where she paid off into reserve during 12.45. OAKLEY languished in Category 'B' Reserve at Portsmouth between 1945-47 and after a refit remained in Category 'A' Reserve at Portsmouth until sold to the Federal German Republic on 11.11.57. In early 1958 she was towed to Liverpool for modernisation by Harland & Wolff. She was finally accepted into the Federal German Navy on 2.10.58 as GNEISENAU, commissioning 16 days later. GNEISENAU served as a gunnery training ship for nearly 20 years before being sold on 12.1.77 for breaking up.

In 11.57 OAKLEY was one of several obsolete British frigates sold to the fledgling navy of the Federal German Republic. Refitted by Harland & Wolff, she was renamed GNEISENAU on 2.10.58. Note the funnel cap, bofors guns and revised radar fit *(W.S.P.L. Kennedy)*

PENYLAN was to have the briefest of careers with the First Destroyer Flotilla. She was lost less than four
months after commissioning on 3.12.42, with heavy loss of life   (N.H.B. 27.8.42)

PENYLAN (L89)

   PENYLAN's active career with the First Destroyer Flotilla lasted just 24 days. After completing her work-
up at Scapa during September and October 1942 and repairing defects on the Thames between 22 October
and 9 November 1942 she was lost on 3.12.42. At 0630 hours on that day whilst escorting Convoy PW257,
she was torpedoed by the German MTB S115 five miles south of Start Point. Five officers and 112 ratings
were rescued.

Launched on 5.11.41 as BOLEBROKE, she was renamed PINDOS on 16.5.42, when she transferred to the
Greeks and spent the whole war in the Mediterranean   (N.H.B. 23.6.42)

Greek PINDOS (ex BOLEBROKE) (L65)

   On 29.1.42 it was agreed that BOLEBROOKE was to be manned by the Royal Hellenic Navy and four months
later on 16.5.42, she was renamed PINDOS and commissioned on 4.6.42.

After working-up at Scapa during July, PINDOS sailed on 12.8.42 as escort for the 28th ML Flotilla from Milford Haven to Gibraltar arriving eight days later. After escorting West African local convoys, PINDOS escorted Convoy WS22 to Durban. She finally arrived at Alexandria on 15.11.42 and immediately joined Operation 'Stoneage' — a convoy escort operation from Alexandria to Malta, with DULVERTON. PINDOS and the convoy arrived at Malta on 17.11.42.

She was to spend the next three months on convoy escort duties in the eastern Mediterranean, between Malta, Tripoli and Alexandria, escorting convoys MW14, MW17, ME11, ME14, ME16 and ME17. She was then allocated to the 5th Destroyer Flotilla on 27.2.43 until 12.44 when she joined the Aegean Escort Flotilla (later the 12th Greek Flotilla) until 5.45. During this period PINDOS was engaged in the Sicily landings; sank U458 with EASTON on 22.8.43 and escorted the PRINCESS ASTRID into Palermo.

PINDOS was also heavily engaged in the abortive Aegean campaign; whilst in company with FAULKNOR and THEMISTOCLES, on 3.10.43 she was unable to engage the German force attacking Kos because of lack of fuel. However she landed stores at Leros on 2.11.43 and again on 3-4.11.43. On 11.11.43 she was bombed but not damaged while approaching Kos harbour and the next day with FAULKNOR and BEAUFORT unsuccessfully searched for German transports. She bombarded enemy positions on Leros on 14.11.43. During 1944, there was much unrest amongst the crew of PINDOS and a mutiny (without casualties) occurred on 5.4.44 and the crew were disarmed after refusing to proceed to sea for Taranto on 12.5.44.

PINDOS was loaned to the Greek Navy until 22.9.59, when it was agreed that she be sold locally in Greece and she was finally discarded during 1960.

PUCKERIDGE closing on an aircraft carrier whilst in the Mediterranean, where she was lost by U-boat attack on 6.9.43
(I.W.M.)

PUCKERIDGE (L108)

Between 9-12.41, PUCKERIDGE was a member of the First Destroyer Flotilla at Portsmouth, undertaking escort duties in the Straits of Dover and the English Channel. On 11.12.41 she was detached to join the Home Fleet for a Norwegian operation and two days later, whilst on passage, she was bombed by a German aircraft off the Pembrokeshire coast. At 0630 hours she was hit by a 250 kg bomb on the quarterdeck between 128-131 frames. The bomb penetrated the vessel and exploded by the after magazine, killing 18 and wounding 20 of her crew in the after messdeck. By 0700 hours, her main engines had re-started and she was steered on her engines towards Milford Haven. The vessel had settled by the stern, with a severe list to starboard, and with her deck awash. By 0810 hours all fires had been extinguished and by 0920 hours a rescue tug had arrived and PUCKERIDGE was towed into Pembroke Dock arriving at 1419 hours. 'Y' mounting had been wrecked and blown over the port side of the ship.

She paid off into Care and Maintenance on 3.1.42 and finally completed her repairs at Pembroke Dock on 10.7.42. After trials, she arrived at Plymouth on 24.7.42 where further modifications were undertaken until 13.8.42. After working-up and acting as an escort for Home Fleet vessels, PUCKERIDGE left Londonderry on

5.10.42 as escort for Convoy WS23 to Freetown where she arrived on the 16th. A week later she left Freetown as escort for the BERGENSFJORD and LEOPOLDVILLE, finally arriving at Gibraltar on 31.10.42.

PUCKERIDGE supported the landing at Oran on 8.11.42 and then escorted follow-up convoys. These duties were interrupted on the 13th when she searched for survivors from the torpedoed Dutch destroyer ISAAC SWEERS. On 13.11.42 she was allocated to the 59th Destroyer Division with which she served until her loss. Beside her usual escort duties, PUCKERIDGE escorted assault convoys for the invasion of Sicily on 10.7.43, and carried out a bombardment of coastal batteries. On 8.8.43, she escorted the liners VULCANIA and SATURNIA from Gibraltar to Malta.

However, on 6.9.43, whilst on passage from Gibraltar to Oran, PUCKERIDGE was torpedoed and sunk by U617, about 40 miles east of Europa Point, Gibraltar. She was hit by two torpedoes in the stern. These exploded her after magazine and blew off her stern, the after-end plating was wrapped over the searchlight platform. PUCKERIDGE sank in eight minutes with the loss of 62 ratings; nine officers and 120 ratings were saved.

PYTCHLEY in the typical configuration of a destroyer of the 21st Destroyer Flotilla in which she served for the whole war
(I.W.M.)

PYTCHLEY (L92)

After working up at Scapa during 11-12.40, PYTCHLEY joined the 21st Destroyer Flotilla, where she was to serve for the whole of the war on east coast escort duties with occasional attachments to the Rosyth Escort Force. She had one detachment to escort Convoy JW53/RA53 to Russia between 15.2.43 and 14.3.43.

Whilst escorting Convoy FN83 with the destroyer VORTIGERN, two miles off Flamborough Head a ground mine (believed to be acoustic) exploded under her stabiliser compartment, at 1113 hours on 21.6.41. Her main engines and turbo generators stopped; all lighting failed and the boilers were forced off their mountings. The hull was corrugated forward of the machinery spaces. Luckily, there were no casualties. At 1425 hours VORTIGERN commenced towing PYTCHLEY into port. She was to be in dockyard hands on the Tyne for six months, and did not commence sea trials until the following December.

On the night of 24-25.10.43, PYTCHLEY was involved in a violent action with German MTBs. Accompanied by the destroyers WORCESTER, EGLINTON, CAMPBELL and MACKAY and the MGBs 609, 610, 607, 603, 315, 327 and ML's 250 and 517, she was protecting Convoy FN160 off Cromer. The convoy was attacked by 32 MTBs from the German 2nd, 4th, 6th and 8th Flotillas. These were driven off by PYTCHLEY, WORCESTER and MACKAY and while the trawler WILLIAM STEPHEN was lost, the German MTBs S63 and S88 were sunk. On 'D' Day, PYTCHLEY was part of the support force for 'Gold Beach'.

She entered reserve in 1946, being in Category 'B' Reserve between 8.46 and 1948, Category 'C' between 1948 and 1953 at Devonport and finally being transferred disarmed to Category III Reserve at Cardiff until 1956. PYTCHLEY arrived at Llanelli on 1.12.56 for breaking up by E. G. Rees.

A war view of QUANTOCK, with her company lined up. She still retains her searchlight

(Brownell Collection)

QUANTOCK (L58)

QUANTOCK commissioned on 28.1.41 and was immediately allocated to the Rosyth Escort Force for the next two years, escorting convoys up and down the east coast of the UK and repelling E-boat and aircraft attacks several times.

On 15.2.43, she arrived at Plymouth en-route for the Mediterranean Fleet as part of the Gibraltar Escort Force and made passage as far as Gibraltar as part of the escort for Convoy OS43. At Gibraltar, QUANTOCK undertook escort and anti-submarine duties with the 56th Destroyer Division until 9.43. Although she engaged several U-boats, none was sunk.

During the Sicilian landings in 7.43, she engaged three MTBs off Augusta on the 27th and all three retired from the action damaged. Four days later with WHEATLAND, she bombarded the coast road near Taormina. After initial escort duties for the Salerno landings on 9.9.43, she gave fire support against a German counter-attack on the 14th. It was at this time that QUANTOCK joined the 56th Destroyer Division at Malta and served on general escort duties until October 1944.

On 15.10.44, she entered Corfu, flying the flag of the British Flag Officer Taranto and the Adriatic and was to serve later in Greek waters during the re-occupation of Greece.

Later, on 3.12.44, QUANTOCK, WILTON and two other destroyers, together with landing craft (gun) and two MTBs bombarded Porto Lussinpiccolo in the northern Adriatic. Three enemy explosive MTBs were destroyed and one damaged. During December QUANTOCK became SO Ship of the 57th Destroyer Division.

On 5.3.45, she left Malta for the UK and reinforced the 16th Destroyer Flotilla at Harwich for the remainder of the European war.

QUANTOCK as the Ecuadorian PRESIDENTE ALFARO following re-fit by White's of Cowes after her transfer on 16.8.55

(W.S.P.L. Kennedy)

QUANTOCK laid-up disarmed at Barrow prior to her purchase by Ecuador in 10.54   *(Ken Royall)*

After conversion into an Air Target Ship, QUANTOCK paid off into reserve at the end of 1945 at Portsmouth, remaining there in Category 'B' Reserve until 1946. She was relegated to 'B2' Reserve between 1946-1948 and Category 'C' Reserve 1948-1953. In 1953 she transferred to Class III Reserve at Barrow in Furness and while lying there was purchased on 18.10.54 by the Government of Ecuador together with MEYNELL and subsequently renamed PRESIDENTE ALFARO. After refitting by White's at Cowes, she was formally transferred to the Ecuadorian Navy at Portsmouth on 16.8.55. She served the Ecuadorians until 1978, when she was stricken from the effective list.

QUORN (L66)
After completing her work-up, QUORN spent a month with the 21st Destroyer Flotilla, before joining the 16th Destroyer Flotilla at Harwich during 12.40. She was to spend the whole of her career with this flotilla on convoy protection, anti-shipping and patrol duties, being damaged three times before her loss. On 1.4.41, she was superficially damaged by two delayed action bombs which exploded 20 yards from the port quarter.

Four months later whilst on passage from Harwich to Chatham on 18.8.41, QUORN exploded a mine 40 yards off her port bow. Some minor indentations occurred between frames 149 and 151 and there was minor machinery damage. Repairs at Chatham took until 13.9.41 to complete.

QUORN in 1940, shortly after commissioning. Note that her foremast is uncluttered by any electronic equipment   *(N.H.B.)*

Her second mining, on 20.4.42, was more serious. QUORN, whilst travelling at 20 knots exploded a mine at 1807 hours $1\frac{1}{2}$ miles east of the Aldborough buoy, on the port side of No 1 boiler room. The ship lost way and took a 5° list to port. Two of her crew were killed and two injured. No 1 boiler room filled immediately to sea level and No 2 boiler had to be shut down. She was towed by the patrol vessel SHEARWATER the 53 miles to Harwich, arriving at 0317 hours on 21.4.42.

Repairs were again effected at Chatham and took until 19.8.42. The hull had been indented from frames 50 to 67 and an area 30 ft × 15 ft had to be replaced; various bulkheads and a part of the keel had also been distorted.

On the night of the 13-14.10.42, QUORN was one of the vessels engaged in the 'KOMET' action. Some 18 months later on the night of 16-17.5.44 she pursued S177, S178, S189, S180 and S179 of the German 2nd MTB Flotilla which had laid 20 mines off Hearty Knoll.

On 3.8.44, QUORN was sunk off the Normandy beaches by a German Linsen explosive boat of the Small Battle Unit Flotilla 211. The explosion occurred on the starboard side amidships and the ship took an immediate 40° list to starboard. In one minute she was on her beam ends, although she temporarily righted herself she had broken in two amidships. Both ends sank rapidly, until about 30 ft of the stern and 15 ft of the bows were above the water. Four officers and 126 ratings were lost. The disaster emphasised the need to fit an additional escape scuttle in the ship's side, immediately aft of the collision bulkhead, to enable trapped personnel to escape.

ROCKWOOD, a Type 3 vessel, had a brief career. She was written off after being severely damaged by an Hs293 glider bomb in the Dodecanese on 11.11.43   *(Brownell Collection)*

ROCKWOOD (L39)

ROCKWOOD's active career lasted 53 weeks. After working-up, she joined the 5th Destroyer Flotilla at Alexandria during 2.43 after a passage via the Cape and served with this flotilla for the whole of her service. ROCKWOOD acted as an escort for the Sicily landings on 10.7.43 and with other members of her flotilla was deeply involved in the Aegean campaign in the autumn of 1943.

On 9.10.43, in company with the destroyer PANTHER, ROCKWOOD escorted the AA cruiser CARLISLE, which was making a sortie into the Aegean to intercept German convoys. The squadron was attacked in Scarpanto Strait by Ju87's of II/StG3. PANTHER was sunk and CARLISLE badly damaged. ROCKWOOD towed CARLISLE to Alexandria, where she was declared a constructive total loss.

On the night of 10-11.11.43, ROCKWOOD with the destroyers PETARD and KRAKOWIAK shelled Calino in the Dodecanese. Whilst returning, ROCKWOOD was severely damaged by an Hs293 glider bomb launched from an aircraft of 5/KG100. The bomb hit the port side upperdeck at the after end of the gearing room and passed through the ship without exploding. The steering gear failed and the ship was steered by her main engines, until the forced lubrication pumps were stopped by the rising water in the gearing room and the main engines had to be stopped. ROCKWOOD was towed into Turkish territorial waters by PETARD and temporary repairs were undertaken which took five days.

ROCKWOOD was then towed the 650 miles to Alexandria. Temporary action damage repairs were started at Alexandria on 1.12.43, but she was then towed to the UK with Convoy MKS40 between 10.2-1.3.44 and laid-up in Category 'B' Reserve at Hartlepool on 7.6.44. She then reduced to Category 'C' Reserve on 20.2.46, while awaiting sale to BISCo. Demolition by J. J. King commenced during 8.46 at Gateshead.

SILVERTON — see KRAKOWIAK

SOUTHDOWN on 24.9.41. Note the plastic armour around the bridge, the bow chaser and the revised band stand for the forward 4" gun mounting
(N.H.B.)

SOUTHDOWN (L25)

SOUTHDOWN arrived at Scapa on 17.11.40 to work-up, prior to joining the 16th Destroyer Flotilla, where she was stationed for the whole of the war. She was, however, attached to the Rosyth Escort Force for most of 1941. Her primary duty was to escort east coast convoys.

SOUTHDOWN was damaged in action twice; the first time being on 4.5.41, when she sustained slight leaks and her steering motors were put out of action. Some three years later, on 13.4.44, she was holed several times above the waterline, which required eight days to repair. She also received collision damage on three occasions on 17.9.41 when she collided with the patrol vessel SHEARWATER off Sheringham and on 5.4.44 and 25.4.44 when she suffered slight collision damage at Parkeston Quay.

Typical of the many minor but violent actions fought by the east coast escorts, were those of the night of 4-5.3.43, when SOUTHDOWN with the destroyer WINDSOR and the patrol vessel SHELDRAKE engaged vessels of the German 2nd, 4th and 6th Flotillas off Lowestoft. Subsequently on 22-23.2.44, GARTH and SOUTHDOWN supported by MTBs 609 and 610 drove off the German 2nd and 8th MTB Flotillas, which attacked the convoy they were protecting off Smith's Knoll. MTBs S94 and S128 collided and were abandoned by the Germans.

94

At the end of the war SOUTHDOWN and BROCKLESBY were the first allied warships to enter Cuxhaven on 14.5.45. On 8.9.45, SOUTHDOWN was designated as an Air Target Ship at Rosyth where her armament was removed over the next month. This duty lasted only a few months as she was relegated to Category 'B' Reserve at Portsmouth on 22.5.46. She was to remain in reserve (at Portsmouth until 1948, Category 'B2' Reserve at Harwich between 1948-50, Category 'C' Reserve in Harwich between 1950-53 and finally Extended reserve at Barrow in Furness between 1953 and 1956), until being scrapped by Ward's at Barrow where work began on 1.11.56.

SOUTHDOWN under demolition at Barrow on 5.11.56 *(Ken Royall)*

SOUTHWOLD (L10)

After completing her trials and work-up, SOUTHWOLD rounded the Cape as a convoy escort calling at Mombasa on 29.12.41 and joined the 5th Destroyer Flotilla at Alexandria during 1.42. She was immediately in action whilst forming part of the escort for Convoy MW9B between 12.2 and 16.2.42 and was present at the Second Battle of Sirte on 20.3.42. She was to survive a mere four days longer, because on 24.3.42, while passing a line to the disabled transport BRECONSHIRE off Malta, a mine exploded under her engine room. One officer and four ratings were killed. All power and electrical services were lost, but the diesel generator was started. The engine room flooded but water flooding into the gearing room was held in check by shoring up the bulkhead and by blocking leaks. A tow was attached to SOUTHWOLD by the tug ANCIENT, but the ship's side plating abreast the engine room split right up to the upper deck on both sides. She sagged and took a list to starboard and the wounded were transferred to DULVERTON. The midship portion gradually sank lower and the ship began to work with the swell that had arisen. She was then abandoned, started to settle with considerable sag and sank later.

STEVENSTONE is seen at Malta post war whilst serving with the 3rd Destroyer Flotilla of the Mediterranean Fleet *(Brownell Collection)*

STEVENSTONE (L16)

On 1.12.42, before she had been completed, it was proposed to transfer STEVENSTONE to the Free French Navy, but the order was rescinded on 23.1.43 and she worked up normally, joining the First Destroyer Flotilla during 5.43. She served with this flotilla on patrol and escort duties until late 1944 when she transferred to the 16th Destroyer Flotilla at Harwich to help protect the newly opened sea lanes to the Belgian and French ports.

STEVENSTONE participated in several actions against German surface vessels. The most famous of these was the disastrous action off the Channel Islands on the night of 23.10.43 when STEVENSTONE with WENSLEYDALE, TALYBONT, LIMBOURNE, GRENVILLE, ROCKET and the cruiser CHARYBDIS were in action against the German torpedo boats T22, T23, T25, T26 and T27. Six months later on the night of the 23-24.4.44 STEVENSTONE, with HALDON and VOLUNTEER, was engaged with vessels of the 4th MTB Flotilla (S146, S147, S145, S167, S130 and S150) off Hastings.

On 'D' Day STEVENSTONE was part of the Support Force for 'Juno' beach. A week later on the night of 12-13.6.44 with the destroyers ISIS and GLAISDALE, she engaged Geman MTBs off Le Havre. S138, S100, S84 and S143 were damaged. On 6.7.44 she picked up the survivors of the frigate TROLLOPE which had been torpedoed at 0123 hours. Soon after her transfer to the 16th Destroyer Flotilla she sank an MTB off Nieuport on the night of 31.10-1.11.44 whilst on patrol duties. A month later on 30.11.44 whilst operating with the frigate STAYNER off Ostend, she was mined at position 51.35 N 03.14 E. The explosion occurred on the starboard side abreast the forward 4″ magazine and STEVENSTONE immediately took a 4° list to starboard and trimmed by the bow, the ship flooding forward of 37 bulkhead. The forward gun was put out of action. Fourteen of her complement were killed and 18 wounded, many of the casualties being due to fires from the explosion of oil fuel and methyl chloride from the cooling system. The explosion centred on frame 30 and the keel plate was pushed in for 20 feet between frame 26 and 37, with a hole about 11 ft long and 12 ft wide. STEVENSTONE arrived at Sheerness on 1.12.44 stern-first accompanied by the tug EUSTON CROSS and the salvage vessel LINCOLN SALVOR. Repairs undertaken on the Thames took six months between 22.12.44 and 28.6.45.

On 3.9.45 STEVENSTONE was acting as reserve for the Far East Fleet and was working-up in the Mediterranean. She remained in the Mediterranean with the 3rd Destroyer Flotilla until later 1947, suffering a slight collision with BRISSENDEN on 20.3.46.

By 31.12.47, she was listed as reducing to reserve at Harwich and was in 'B1' Reserve at Harwich between 1948/49. After docking and a hull survey at Chatham between 16.9.48 and 13.11.48 she was repaired there between 17.1.49 and 2.12.49.

STEVENSTONE was to remain in reserve (Category 'C' at Chatham in 1949/50, at Harwich in 1950/52, returning to Chatham in 1952/53 and finally at Hartlepool between 1953/8). On 13.11.58 approval was given for her to be down-graded to Extended Reserve and scrapped. On 2.9.59 STEVENSTONE was towed from Hartlepool to the Dunston yard of Clayton and Davie for demolition.

TALYBONT, was the last Hunt to complete in 5.43, as her completion had been delayed by the bombing of White's yard at Cowes   (N.H.B.)

TALYBONT (L18)

TALYBONT was the last Hunt to complete as her builder's yard at Cowes had been bombed heavily and her completion delayed. After working-up at Scapa, she finally joined the 15th Destroyer Flotilla at Plymouth on 12.7.43 with which she was to serve for the next 15 months on patrol and escort duties. TALYBONT participated in the CHARYBDIS action. She received damage about the waterline when she collided with a merchant ship on 2.12.43 which necessitated four weeks repairs at Devonport.

On 5.2.44, TALYBONT, with TANATSIDE, BRISSENDEN and WENSLEYDALE was in action with the German torpedo boat T29 and minesweepers M156 and M206 off the north coast of Brittany. M156 was badly damaged and was later destroyed by air attacks at L'Abervrac'h.

On 'D' Day, she was part of the Support Force for 'Omaha Beach' and was slightly damaged by near misses and splinters from shore batteries off Cap Levi on 17.6.44, 1.7.44 and finally on 3.7.44. Her final action of the war was on the night of 23-24.8.44, when with the frigate THORNBOROUGH and MTBs 692, 694 and 695, she damaged the German vessels V716 and R229 which were attempting to escape from Le Havre.

After joining the 16th Destroyer Flotilla during 10.44, TALYBONT collided with a merchant ship on 9.11.44, and was holed on the port side of the quarter deck between frames 122-134 from the upper deck to below the waterline. Repairs at Chatham lasted two months.

TALYBONT then resumed her patrol and escort duties until 5.45. After extra ballast had been fitted between 26.6.-2.7.45, she sailed for refit at Malta in preparation for service in the Far East. She was still refitting in

TALYBONT was another Hunt to see post-war service with the 3rd Flotilla of the Mediterranean Fleet between 1945-1947   (Brownell Collection)

'VJ' Day and formed part of the 6th Destroyer Division of the Mediterranean Fleet until 1947. On 19.1.47, she damaged herself once more, when she collided with a wreck whilst securing to the main breakwater at Haifa. Her side was pushed in and holed between frames 80 and 87 and she was under repair at Malta until May.

By 31.12.47, TALYBONT had reduced to reserve at Portsmouth and was to remain in reserve until her disposal. Between 1947 and 11.49 she was in Category 'B1' Reserve at Portsmouth, refitting at Liverpool until 2.50, Category 'B' 1950/1 and Category 'C' in 1951/2 at Harwich. On 7.11.52, it was agreed that TALYBONT was to be laid-up in a state of preservation by Kindberg's Ltd at the Coal Dock, West Hartlepool. Between 1952/5, she was in Class II Reserve and then dropped to Extended Reserve until 2.61. Between 11.56 and 1960 she was used as a Harbour Training Ship for Artificers at Rosyth, until relieved by the destroyer CHEVIOT.

TALYBONT was towed to Shipbreaking Industries yard at Charlestown for demolition, arriving on 14.2.61. Fifteen months later on 3.5.62 a letter from BISCo confirmed that demolition had been completed. Her net scrap realisation was £19,950.

TANATSIDE (L69)

While working-up near Scapa, TANATSIDE was damaged in a collision with the minesweeper BRAMBLE on 26.9.42 in position 58.43 N 03.18 E which necessitated a month's repair on the Tyne until 28.10.42. After completing her work-up, she joined the 15th Destroyer Flotilla at Plymouth serving for the next two years on patrol and escort duties. A collision with the merchant ship NORMANVILLE on 23.10.43 resulted in five weeks repair at Devonport to replace her damaged stem and forecastle plating.

Whilst primarily engaged on escort and patrol duties, TANATSIDE was in action against enemy forces on 5.2.44 when she was slightly damaged by a 40 mm shell, fired by an enemy MTB which exploded at the level of the wheelhouse. She was soon repaired and was part of the Support Force for 'Omaha Beach' on 6.6.44, but returned to Bristol to refit between 17.7. and 22.9.44.

Seen during 11.42, shortly after commissioning, TANATSIDE subsequently became the R.H.N. ADRIAS (II) on 12.2.46 and served with the Greeks until 1962
(N.H.B.)

During 12.44, she was transferred to the 21st Flotilla at Sheerness and had only been on station a few days, when she collided with the frigate BYRON on 16.12.44. The collision caused a 10 ft horizontal split from her stem along her waterline and her stem below water was pushed to port. Repairs were completed at Devonport on 22.1.45.

TANATSIDE remained on station until the European war ended and after making passage to the Mediterranean, she started a refit and alterations at Taranto on 16.7.45 in anticipation of further service in the Far East. The refit was not completed, and in 11.45 she was listed as being under care and maintenance at Taranto. On the fifth of that month she was offered to the Greeks as a replacement for ADRIAS (I) under the terms of the Anglo-Hellenic Loan of Ships Agreement. TANATSIDE was finally transferred to the Royal Hellenic Navy at Malta on 12.2.46 and became the ADRIAS (II). She was to serve with the Greeks until 10.8.62, when she transferred to the Royal Navy in Greece for de-equipping. ADRIAS (II) was formally discarded in 1963 and sold for scrap locally on 14.1.64.

TETCOTT (L99)

TETCOTT was seriously damaged in a collision with the corvette HEARTSEASE on 23.12.41 while working-up, and this necessitated repairs on the Clyde and at Southampton until 9.3.42. After completing her work-up, TETCOTT joined the 5th Destroyer Flotilla at Alexandria taking passage with Convoy WS18 via the Cape in time to participate in the 'Vigorous' Malta convoy action between 12-16.6.42. She rescued 79 survivors from her sister GROVE on the 12th. TETCOTT remained in the Mediterranean until the end of the European war, serving with 22nd Flotilla after 11.43.

TETCOTT with CROOME, SIKH and ZULU participated in the sinking of U372 off the Palestine coast on 4.8.42. She was also present as an escort for the Sicily, Salerno and Anzio landings besides her usual escort and patrol duties.

TETCOTT was seriously damaged in a collision when working-up but survived the war
(Brownell Collection)

After returning to Portsmouth to give leave and to undertake repairs, she was taken in hand for a refit at Gibraltar on 5.7.45. However, the end of the Japanese war caused her to be reduced to Category 'B' Reserve at Portsmouth on 17.1.46, remaining there until 1952. On 3.4.48 she was reclassified as 'A1' Reserve, but three months later on 29.7.48 she reduced to 'A2' Reserve. On 4.11.52, it was announced that TETCOTT would be laid-up in a state of preservation at the Penarth Pontoon, Slipway and Ship Repairing Co Ltd in Penarth Docks. However, in 1953, she was towed to Gibraltar and remained there for some two years. In 9.55, she was towed to Barrow in Furness and relegated to Extended Reserve. On 6.1.56 she was downgraded to the

Another view of TETCOTT, whilst laid-up in reserve at Barrow, prior to her demolition in 9.56. Notice all her equipment has been cocooned but the vessel is in poor condition   *(Ken Royall)*

status of a hulk and was no longer regarded as being part of the Reserve Fleet. Eight months later, on 10.8.56, after all her valuable equipment had been removed, the vessel was made available to BISCo for disposal. TETCOTT was towed from Barrow on 22.9.56 and arrived at Ward's Milford Haven yard two days later for demolition. On 9.4.57 BISCo confirmed that demolition had been completed.

TYNEDALE (L96)

TYNEDALE arrived at Portsmouth on 27.12.40 and served with the First Destroyer Flotilla until late 1941, when she joined the 15th Destroyer Flotilla at Plymouth until her deployment to the Mediterranean in 4.43. Whilst in the Mediterranean she served with the 59th Destroyer Division until September and then with the 57th Destroyer Division until her loss.

TYNEDALE was generally employed on convoy and escort duties but on 11.3.41, she was slightly damaged by three bombs that exploded underwater — one abreast the engine room and two abreast No 1 gun — whilst she was berthed alongside the Pitch House Jetty, Portsmouth. The ship was out of action for nine days.

A year later, on the night of the 27-28.3.42, she was one of the escorts for vessels undertaking the raid on St Nazaire. She was slightly damaged in collision with the WAR NIZAM on 28.9.42 and on the night of 13-14.10.42, she was in action against the raider 'KOMET' in the Channel.

After TYNEDALE had joined the Mediterranean Fleet, she participated in Operation 'Husky'. She was damaged by two near misses whilst in Augusta harbour, her speed was reduced to 15 knots and her Type 285 fire control radar was put out of action. This damage necessitated repairs at Gibraltar between 21.8 and 18.9.43.

TYNEDALE during 11.42, whilst serving with the 15th Destroyer Flotilla at Plymouth *(N.H.B.)*

Whilst escorting Convoy KMS34 in the Gulf of Bougie at position 37.10 N 06.05 E, TYNEDALE was torpedoed by U593 at 1710 hours on 12.12.43. The torpedo struck TYNEDALE amidships, breaking the vessel in half. The bow portion sank quickly with few survivors, but the stern portion remained afloat for a short while and most of the crew there were rescued. The survivors were picked up by the corvette HYDERABAD and the rescue tug HENGIST. Sixty-six crew members were lost.

WENSLEYDALE (L86)

WENSLEYDALE's short active career of two years was largely spent with the 15th Destroyer Flotilla at Plymouth from 12.42 until 9.44 prior to a final brief period with the 21st Destroyer Flotilla at Sheerness.

During her service with the 15th Flotilla, WENSLEYDALE participated in several actions against German surface vessels, the most important of which was the CHARYBDIS action of 23.10.43. Other actions occurred on the night of 28-29.5.43, when WENSLEYDALE sustained damage to her torpedo tubes in an action against German MTBs; and again on 10.7.43 when she was damaged slightly in action against torpedo boats and MTBs. Her final surface engagement was on 5.2.44, when with TALYBONT, TANATSIDE and BRISSENDEN, she was in action against German torpedo boats and minesweepers.

In the summer of 1944, WENSLEYDALE participated in the sinking of U671 on 4.8.44 and U413 on 20.8.44, both in the Channel. However, during her career she was involved in two collisions, the second of which was to result in her being declared a constructive total loss. The first collision on 3.7.44 was with a tug when she suffered a split in the ship's side approximately 2' 6" long, 2 feet above the upper deck level between frames six and nine on her port side. The second collision occurred on 21.11.44 and involved LST 367. The port side and upper deck plating of WENSLEYDALE from frame 88 to 98 was indented and fractured to a depth of 6 ft on the upper deck. The engine room and gearing room were flooded and open to the sea.

WENSLEYDALE's reduction to Category 'C' Reserve on 17.12.44 and subsequent disposal was probably due to a combination of the Royal Navy manning crisis and to the damage being sustained so late in the war.

WENSLEYDALE was upgraded to Category 'B' Reserve on 28.2.45, which would suggest that the intention was to repair her, however, nine months later, on 8.11.45, she was approved for scrapping. In 6.3.46 she was reduced to Category 'C' Reserve at West Hartlepool and three months later on 29.6.46 she was placed on the sale list. On 25.2.47, WENSLEYDALE arrived at the yard of Hughes Bolckow at Blyth for breaking up.

WENSLEYDALE during 12.42 shortly after completion. She was to be the sole marine loss of the Hunts, being written off after collision with an L.S.T. during 11.44 *(N.H.B.)*

WHADDON on 13.6.42, 16 months after she first commissioned and whilst serving with the Rosyth Escort Force *(N.H.B.)*

WHADDON (L45)

WHADDON's first two years service with the Rosyth Escort Force was as an escort for convoys along the east coast. She received superficial damage from bomb splinters whilst lying at Hull on 8.5.41 — the only damage she received in service.

WHADDON was then allocated to the Mediterranean Fleet and sailed as an additional escort for Convoy KMF11 on 18.3.43, joining the 60th Destroyer Division with which she served until the end of the war. During her Mediterranean service, WHADDON undertook escort and patrol duties and also participated in the amphibious landings at Pantellaria (10-11.6.43), Sicily, Salerno and finally the South of France landings between 9-14.8.44.

Between 20-24.9.44, she and BELVOIR were in action against the three German torpedo boats TA37, TA38 and TA39 which were on passage from Trieste to the Aegean. An indecisive action took place in the Straits of Otranto. After refitting at Alexandria between 1-2.45. WHADDON operated in the Adriatic during the following month.

After again refitting at Gibraltar between 5.6. and 17.7.45, she sailed from there on 29.9.45 en-route to Devonport to reduce to reserve. She was to remain in reserve from 10.45-4.59 when she was towed to Faslane for scrapping by Shipbreaking Industries, arriving there on 5.4.59. She had been laid-up in Category 'B' Reserve until 1948, Category 'C' between 1948-53 and Category III in 1953/4. In 1954, she had been towed to Cardiff from Devonport and reduced to Extended Reserve there until her disposal.

A war view of WHEATLAND. Again the searchlight is still fitted   *(I.W.M.)*

WHEATLAND (L122)

On completion of her work-up, WHEATLAND was attached to the Home Fleet for the Lofoten raid. She returned early from the raid as escort for the damaged landing ship PRINCESS CHARLOTTE. On her return she transferred to the Portsmouth Command for three months of escort duties, before again transferring to the 8th Destroyer Flotilla of the Home Fleet until 10.42.

Her principal duty during this period was to escort the fleet covering Russian convoys or the convoys themselves. In 5.42 she had escorted the damaged battleship KING GEORGE V from Iceland to the UK, returning to Iceland to escort the battleship DUKE OF YORK which was then covering Convoys PQ16 and QP12. She returned to Scapa on the 29th. Between 28.6.42 and her return to Scapa on 8.7.42, she escorted the DUKE OF YORK which was then covering the ill-fated convoy PQ17 to Russia.

After repairs at Hull between 22.7. and 20.8.42, WHEATLAND rejoined the Home Fleet and with WILTON escorted the escort carrier AVENGER which was acting a close escort to Convoy PQ18 which had sailed from Loch Ewe on 2.9.42. Thirteen out of 40 vessels in the convoy were lost but the remainder reached North Russia safely and the close escort, WHEATLAND included, escorted the return convoy PQ15 home with the loss of three more merchant ships, two escorts and an oiler.

In 11.42, she was allocated to the Mediterranean, and remained there until the end of the European war, serving with the 57th Destroyer Division until 6.44 and thereafter with the 22nd Destroyer Flotilla. Initially WHEATLAND escorted the headquarters ship BULOLO for the attack on Algiers on 8.11.42 and four days later landed troops at Bone with LAMERTON. WHEATLAND spent the ensuing months on escort duties, sinking with EASTON the Italian submarine ASTERIA north-west of Bougie on 17.2.43 and six days later sank U443 off Algiers whilst operating with LAMERTON, BICESTER and WILTON.

After the landings at Pantellaria 11.6.43, she acted as an escort for the Sicily and Salerno landings, before undertaking local escort duties between Naples and Augusta until 8.44. In that month, she was attached as escort for the covering force for the South of France landings, before undertaking patrol and escort duties in the Adriatic. There, on the night of 1-2.11.44 with AVON VALE, she sank the German torpedo-boat TA20 and corvettes UJ202 and UJ208 south of Lussino. Three officers and 68 ratings were taken prisoner. A fortnight later she bombarded Bar in Jugoslavia and observed several hits.

WHEATLAND refitted at Taranto between 26.3.-20.7.45 and returned to the UK in 8.45 to give leave as she had been allocated to the East Indies Fleet. However, the capitulation of Japan on 2.9.45 meant that WHEATLAND entered Category 'B' Reserve at Devonport during that month. She remained at Devonport until 1953; reducing to Category 'B2' Reserve between 1946-48 before reverting to Category 'B'. After a short sojourn at Penarth, WHEATLAND was towed to Gibraltar in 9.53 and remained there in reserve until 8.55, when she was towed home and used as part of the artificial harbour at Harwich. She was handed over to BISCo and scrapping was commenced by P & W MacLellan at Bo'ness on 20.9.57.

Originally commissioned on 2.42, WILTON is seen when commissioned post war as a member of the 4th Training Flotilla   *(W.S.P.L.)*

WILTON (L128)

On completion, WILTON joined the 8th Destroyer Flotilla of the Home Fleet and saw arduous service in the Arctic and the Mediterranean. After being damaged by ice while covering Convoy PQ14 to Russia during 4.42, she spent from 22.4. to 19.5.42 under repair on the Thames. She then returned to cover further Russian convoys between 5-7.42. In addition she escorted a minelaying operation in the Denmark Strait. WILTON also participated in the 'Pedestal' Convoy between 11-13.8.42 and after being dive-bombed nine times between 11-12.8.42, she was ordered to escort the cruiser NIGERIA, previously torpedoed by a U-boat on 12.8.42, back to Gibraltar. During September 1942, WILTON was one of the escorts for the escort carrier AVENGER protecting Convoy PQ18 en-route to Russia.

On 2.11.42, WILTON with WHEATLAND arrived on detachment to Gibraltar and six days later she was one of the escorts covering the landings at Algiers. The next day, WILTON was very lucky to escape loss as a torpedo passed directly underneath her. Eight days later on 11.11.42, she participated in the Bougie landings and was later employed escorting convoys to and from Algiers. She participated in the sinking of U443 off Algiers on 23.2.43 when operating with her sisters BICESTER, LAMERTON and WHEATLAND.

WILTON had joined the 57th Destroyer Division in 11.42 and served mainly on routine escort duties until 3.45. She did however participate in the Cape Bon blockade of 5.43; the Salerno landings on 9.9.43 and the sinking of U223 with the destroyers LAFOREY (lost), ULSTER, TUMULT, HAMBLEDON and BLENCATHRA on the night of 29-30.3.44.

In 10.44, she supported army operations on the Albanian coast, aiding the army in the capture of Sarande and Corfu, by bombarding the enemy batteries there on the 4th, 6th and 8th of the month. On 3.12.44, WILTON with three other destroyers, two landing craft and two MTBs bombarded the island of Lussinpiccolo in the Adriatic destroying an enemy explosive motor-boat base. A fortnight later she returned to bombard Fort Asino.

In 3.45 she returned to the UK and joined the 21st Destroyer Flotilla at the Nore for the next three months, before being assigned to Plymouth and allocated to the East Indies Fleet.

WILTON then made passage to Simonstown where she refitted between 28.8.45 and 8.1.46. She then returned to Plymouth on 10.2.46 and immediately reduced to Category 'B' Reserve at Devonport until 12.49. She was to spend the next two years as a unit of the 4th Training Flotilla at Rosyth and after a period as an Air Target Ship, reduced to Class 2 Reserve at Devonport between 1952/53. In 1953, WILTON was transferred to Cardiff and remained in reserve there as Senior Ship to the South Wales Reserve Fleet (between 1953/55 she was in Class 2 Reserve and after that time in Extended Reserve until late 1959). On 4.12.59, WILTON arrived at Faslane to be broken-up by Shipbreaking Industries. Her net scrap realisation was £22,900. It is believed that she was the last active Hunt apart from BROCKLESBY in the Royal Navy.

Two views of ZETLAND taken during the war *(Top N.H.B. 9.42. Bottom W.S.P.L.).* Post war, she became the Norwegian TROMSO in 1954

ZETLAND (L59)

ZETLAND's first five months of service with the Londonderry Special Escort Division were particularly active. After joining the convoy for Operation 'Pedestal' which sailed from the Clyde on 3.8.42, she refuelled at Gibraltar a week later and formed part of the escort for Force Z, the support force for the convoy. She returned to Gibraltar on 14.8.42 as escort for the battleship RODNEY.

After leaving Gibraltar on the 16th with RODNEY, ZETLAND was detached to support Convoy SL118 which was under heavy U-boat attack three days later. However, on 21.8.42, ZETLAND and the Polish BLYSKAWICA were detached from SL118 to escort the torpedoed AMC CHESHIRE into Belfast. She then escorted Convoys WS22, SL119 and RMS QUEEN ELIZABETH as well as units of the Home Fleet between Scapa, Rosyth and the Clyde.

Subsequently escort work from Londonderry was curtailed by damage to her Asdic dome that necessitated docking at Greenock. ZETLAND left Londonderry for Gibraltar on 28.10.42 and undertook inshore duties on 8.11.42 when the landings were made at Algiers. ZETLAND opened fire at the fort on Cape Matifa, extinguishing a searchlight. Later that day, ZETLAND took the destroyer BROKE in tow when the latter returned from her assault on the boom at Algiers harbour. The two ships collided during the towing operations, and the BROKE, which had been badly damaged, sank the next day, her crew being rescued by ZETLAND.

ZETLAND remained with the 57th Destroyer Division as part of the Inshore Squadron until 31.5.43, participating in the rescue of survivors from the corvette SAMPHIRE which had been sunk by a U-boat whilst escorting Convoy TE14 on 30.1.43 and in the sinking of a small enemy vessel 30 miles north-east of Cape Bon on 9.5.43. However, ZETLAND was now suffering from an accumulation of damage resulting from near

misses and her collision with the BROKE and arrived on the Tyne for refit on 7.6.43. This refit and repair at Palmer's Jarrow yard lasted until 16.8.43 and after working-up, she sailed from Londonderry a month later and joined the 59th Destroyer Division at Malta. Her duties were to escort convoys to and from the east coast of Italy and patrols off the Dalmation coast. On the night of 2-3.12.43, ZETLAND was damaged in the air raid on Bari, during which 17 ships were lost, and was under repair at Taranto until 15.1.44.

In the next months, the only noteworthy incidents in her career were to shell, with LAUDERDALE (qv), a searchlight position on the approaches to Dubrovnik on the night of 12-13.4.44 and to participate in the South of France landings. Between 9.44 and 1.45, ZETLAND was engaged in operations in the Aegean and with LIDDESDALE and BRECON entered Pegadia Bay on Scarpanto and sank a caique and silenced enemy shore batteries.

Although she was allocated to the Eastern Fleet on returning to Harwich on 4.2.45, she was temporarily attached to the 16th Destroyer Flotilla with which she remained until 6.45. During this period, in company with other ships she had several clashes with German MTBs.

ZETLAND refitted at Alexandria between 25.6. and 2.10.45 and as she was no longer required for Far East Service she returned to the UK during 10.45. After service with the local flotilla, she entered Category 'B' Reserve at Portsmouth on 20.4.46. She later reduced to Category 'C' Reserve until 2.9.54 when she was loaned to the Royal Norwegian Navy as TROMSO. She was sold outright to the Norwegians in 1956 and was broken up locally in 1965.

ZETLAND in tow in Portsmouth Harbour in 1952   *(W.S.P.L. Kennedy)*

ROYAL NAVY PENDANT NUMBERS AS COMPLETED

L03 Badsworth	L39 Rockwood	L73 Melbreak
L05 Atherstone	L42 Brocklesby	L74 Middleton
L06 Avon Vale	L43 Blackmore	L75 Haydon
L07 Airedale	L44 Glaisdale	L76 Brecon
L08 Burton/Exmoor (II)	L45 Whaddon	L77 Grove
L09 Easton	L46 Cleveland	L78 Cottesmore
L10 Southwold	L47 Blean	L79 Brissenden
L11 Fernie	L48 Holderness	L81 Catterick
L12 Albrighton	L50 Bleasdale	L82 Meynell
L14 Beaufort	L51 Bramham/Themistocles	L83 Derwent
L15 Eggesford	L52 Cowdray	L84 Hursley/Kriti
L16 Stevenstone	L53 Kanaris/Hatherleigh	L85 Heythrop
L17 Berkeley	L54 Cotswold	L86 Wensleydale
L18 Talybont	L56 Holcombe	L87 Eglinton
L19 Haldon/La Combattante	L57 Limbourne	L88 Lamerton
L20 Garth	L58 Quantock	L89 Penylan
L22 Aldenham	L59 Zetland	L90 Ledbury
L24 Blencathra	L60 Mendip	L91 Miaoulis (Modbury)
L25 Southdown	L61 Exmoor (I)	L92 Pytchley
L26 Bedale/Slazak	L62 Croome	L95 Lauderdale
L27 Goathland	L63 Dulverton	L96 Tynedale
L28 Hurworth	L65 Pindos (Bolebroke)	L98 Oakley (II) (ex Tickham)
L30 Blankney	L66 Quorn	L99 Tetcott
L31 Chiddingfold	L67 Adrias (Border)	L100 Liddesdale
L32 Belvoir	L68 Eridge	L108 Puckeridge
L34 Bicester	L69 Tanatside	L115 Silverton/Krakowiak
L35 Cattistock	L70 Farndale	L122 Wheatland
L36 Eskdale	L71 Calpe	L128 Wilton
L37 Hambledon	L72 Oakley (I)/Kujawiak	

On the reclassification of the remaining ships as frigates in 1947, the Flag Superior changed to F and most vessels either retained their original number or had 100 added to their former L Superior number, e.g. BICESTER (F134). However SILVERTON (F55) was re-numbered, AVON VALE added 200 to her original number, whilst WHEATLAND had 100 deducted from her original number.

VALDEMAR SEJR (ex EXMOOR (II)) after her refit. Note the lattice mast, the revised anti-aircraft armament and radar fit
(W.S.P.L. Kennedy)

INDEX TO SHIP HISTORIES AND PHOTOGRAPHS

The Norwegian NARVIK at the Coronation Review. Note the breakwater, modified bridge, up-rated radars, lattice mast and the single bofors for short-range defence   *(N.M.M)*

ALBRIGHTON and GARTH laid up at Barrow   *(Ken Royall)*